BEAUTIFUL BREAD

Create & Bake Artful Masterpieces for Any Occasion

Theresa Culletto

ROCK POINT

© 2023 by Quarto Publishing Group USA, Inc.
Text © 2023 by Theresa Culletto

First published in 2023 by Rock Point, an imprint of The Quarto Group,
142 West 36th Street, 4th Floor, New York, NY 10018, USA
T (212) 779-4972 F (212) 779-6058 www.Quarto.com

Rock Point titles are also available at discount for retail, wholesale, promotional and bulk purchase. For details, contact the Special Sales Manager by email at specialsales@quarto.com or by mail at The Quarto Group, Attn: Special Sales Manager, 100 Cummings Center Suite, 265D, Beverly, MA 01915, USA.

10 9 8 7 6 5 4 3 2

ISBN: 978-1-63106-846-1

Library of Congress Control Number: 2023933030

Publisher: Rage Kindelsperger
Creative Director: Laura Drew
Editorial Director: Erin Canning
Managing Editor: Cara Donaldson
Cover Design: Laura Drew
Interior Layout: Silverglass Design
Photography: Jocelyn Filley

Printed in China

To my sons, Benjamin, Camden, Jacob, and Gordon, who spent many a hot summer helping out in our little cottage bakery packaging breads into the late, late hours, rising early in the morning to work at the farmers market, cleaning up a thousand spilled twisty ties, and eating the crunchies off the trays and calling it dinner. Whew, we made it! How could I have done all of it without you? I love you.

To Aurora and Ella, you put the "grand" in "granddaughters."

Contents

Introduction

Baking bread is transformative, turning the kitchen into a space of pure bliss as its warm aroma beckons throughout the house. Creating bread can be intoxicating, from the suppleness of the dough in your hands to the crisp crackle of the crust. Homemade bread is not only nourishing to the body but also to the soul.

My goal with *Beautiful Bread* is to make the process enjoyable for you. The first, and most important, step for any baking endeavor is to have a little understanding of what you're in for. Recipes that say they're "easy" or "quick," especially concerning bread, are clearly misleading the baker. From the hunting and gathering of tools and ingredients, to the preparation and assembling, to the baking and cleanup, there is nothing quick or easy in producing a good-quality baked good. With any recipe, it's all relative to one's experience in their kitchen, not the author's. I could say all the focaccia dough recipes in this book are easy, but I have been baking bread for over forty years. The truth is, I don't know your skills in the kitchen, so we will take it step by step, see what happens, and, most importantly, have fun, enjoying the process along the way, and with the inspiration of this book, you will discover your own skills as a baker and evoke your inner van Dough.

What Is Artisan Bread?

In general terms, artisan breads are rustic breads that have been made by hand by a skilled baker. Focaccia is a rustic, folksy kind of artisan bread made by hand. It's rustic because it is made with few ingredients and can easily be baked outside over a hot fire on a stone. It's folksy because it is handcrafted in the traditional manner with a new artistic flare. If this is your first time making bread, focaccia is an excellent starting place. You will soon understand the difference between real artisan bread and that only labeled as artisan bread. Please allow yourself space to try and try again; success will come.

What Is Bread Art?

Artisan focaccia tastes amazing and looks inviting on its own; however, by adding simple ingredients arranged in a creative design on your flatbread, you will bring this traditional bread into an artisanal space that pleases all the senses. The bread projects in this book are created with fresh vegetables, fruits, and herbs, making them nutritious too. A colorful array of mini sweet peppers, red onions, and salty brined olives placed on focaccia dough can transform bread into a strikingly beautiful work of art, full of vibrant colors, tastes, and textures that represent your own creative expression. I can't envision a more artistic way to eat our daily veggies and fruits. Plus, bread art is always a crowd-pleaser at parties. To those who are interested, most of the recipes and bread art projects in this book are vegan friendly.

What Do You Need to Get Started?

Limited space and resources are not a problem for making these types of breads. Just a few kitchen tools and a very hot oven are all you need to create good-quality artisan bread. I like to use as few tools as necessary, making as little mess as possible, seeing as I am the one who is cleaning it up. The simple process for preparing most of the focaccia dough recipes in this book is the one-bowl, no-flour-on-the-counter method known as the stretch-and-fold technique (page 19), which has been around longer than I originally thought. I was taught this "new" method by Peter Reinhart, who called it a real game changer; however, being the ever-consummate cookbook reader, I later discovered a few bread recipes from a very old bread cookbook that describe this very method for creating strong bread doughs. There are a few times when you will need to dust the work surface with flour and get both hands dirty. While you can make any of the dough recipes in a stand mixer, I highly recommend working these recipes by hand, both to familiarize yourself with dough textures and changes in the dough, as well as for the therapy. There is something so soothing about working soft, supple dough with your hands that puts you into a state of mindful relaxation. Good quality bread requires time, also teaching us patience. You don't have to run out and buy new tools; I suggest working with what you have—look around and open the utility or utensil drawer. Creativity is born out of necessity.

How to Find Inspiration?

While this cookbook shares specific designs for your focaccia bread art, consider it practice for future focaccia art you will create on your own. Special occasions are made memorable with something extraordinarily beautiful that you have created. Here, you will learn the best techniques for baking dough and cutting and handling decorations, along with a few bonus recipes to serve with your breads. Finding inspiration for your own designs is entirely yours to explore. My very first focaccia bread art

project was inspired by a highway, of all things, on a trip to North Carolina (see Poppy Field on page 46). What does it take to be inspired? A walk in the woods, a tour of a museum, vacation photos, a good book, or perhaps a memory drawn from your own personal experiences and imagination. I find nature to be the purest form of inspiration. The colors that illuminate our world are always in perfect harmony and often found just beyond our doors. Being outside brings a spontaneous feeling of awe and awareness, awakening all our senses and sparking creativity naturally. Daily walks outside are one of the simplest ways to discover new colors and textures and be inspired.

How to Create Bread Art?

Once you have tried a few projects in this book, you may want to create your own bread art. I highly recommend that you make a sketch of your idea ahead of time. Most of the projects in this book came from a drawing. You don't have to be an artist; just jot down on paper approximate placement and shapes you are hoping to achieve with your vegetables and herbs on your focaccia. Having a sketch helps to move along in the process.

The number-one thing you will hear once you do create bread art is that "It's too beautiful to cut." Simply respond with "No worries, there's more where that came from," which will be true. Once you have completed one work of focaccia art, it may just become a favorite kitchen project and your go-to dish for occasions. You will be the talk at the neighbor's cookout, or the next conference-room luncheon (in a good way). The more you practice, the better you will be. The therapy of art and baking combined is, in itself, beneficial to the mind, body, and soul.

Making Bread Art

If you have never tried to bake bread or don't feel confident about baking with yeast, as stated earlier, focaccia is the perfect place to start. Flatbreads, more specifically focaccia, are an excellent entry point for new bread bakers. Focaccia breads require minimal preparation and shaping. I have formulated these recipes to easily be worked by hand. Each one is a little over 2 pounds, or 1 kilogram. As a baking artist, you will create your own canvas, and like a canvas, you will stretch the dough onto a baking sheet where beautiful works of art will be created. Though these breads become masterpieces, they are meant to be enjoyed both visually and as part of a meal.

WHAT ABOUT GLUTEN-FREE BREAD?

I did not forget about gluten-free. There are times when even experienced bakers fail at recipes and are humbled through trial and error, spending countless hours experimenting and ending up with half bags of gluten-free ingredients. I have tried my very best to create a gluten-free dough that would be suitable and taste amazing, but I still have not been able to achieve or come close to that amazing flavor and structure the protein of wheat imparts to bread. I have been humbled. However, if you have a favorite recipe that works well for you, feel free to skip on over to the project sections of this book using your own recipe.

The Rise and Fall of Dough

Dough waits for no one. Once flour, water, and yeast are mixed, it's lights, camera, action, you're on! The average time to develop a ripe flavorful dough is 2 hours, start to finish, give or take, depending on your environment. Getting your produce prepped right after you mix the dough is a good multitask moment. Doing a mock layout of your design on a spare piece of parchment is also a time-saver. This helps to transition quickly to the dough when it is shaped and ready to decorate. Watch the dough as you are setting up your design for signs of over-ripening or the "fall" (page 18). Dough will start to wrinkle and draw back into itself; it may become wet and sticky or too dry. A doughy residue on the side of the bowl where the dough once clung is a clue that the dough has over-ripened. Warmer workspaces will make for a very active rise. If it appears to be deflating or falling, deflate it all the way, reshape it into a tight ball, cover, and pop it into the refrigerator. This will slow down the process while you finish the vegetable prep and setup.

Decorations

Vegetables, fruits, seeds, and nuts provide food artists with an entire palette of colors. Luckily for us, there is a whole world of color at grocery stores and farmers markets, and even in our crisper drawers. Use those colors! These works of art are made for two purposes: one is to enjoy with the eyes, and the other is to enjoy with a passionate appetite and good cheeses, wine, and assorted spreads, oils, and dips. A word of caution: Your toppings should never weigh more than half the weight of your dough. For the most part, a bread dough is slightly over 2 pounds (1 kg) for the best texture and baking response on the bread. Keeping your toppings to about half or a little less of that weight will provide the perfect balance. In this book, I give you step-by-step guidance on some beautiful focaccia art projects, and you can take it from there. Keep in mind that the color of anything you bake is going to change with the heat. Eggplant goes from that beautiful purple plum to dark brown, peppers turn darker, and onions brown slightly on the edges. It's just a matter of making those colors work in your art piece. Nuts turn very dark due to all the oil. Basil burns easily because of its thin leafy membranes. See the sections on nuts and herbs (page 12) for tips on how to keep colors fresh while baking.

Baking in an Oven

It all comes down to the bake. I have used many ovens in many houses and locations and each one is calibrated differently. From commercial to household, they all have their own variables. Oven controls marked Fahrenheit, Celsius, or gas mark in conventional, convection, gas, or electric all make baking happen but not always in the same timing or temperature settings. Use temperatures and baking times referenced in this cookbook as a guide, not gospel. Your oven is going to dictate a perfect bake. Keep a kitchen notebook and pen handy to make notes for the next time or jot them down next to the recipe in the cookbook.

Ways to Serve Bread Art

Most of the bread art in this book is centerpiece-worthy and will elevate any meal or occasion. Beautiful focaccia is perfect for a large gathering, a themed party, a charcuterie spread, or even a birthday party cake substitute and serves six to eight people. As part of a buffet, it can remain whole, placed on a large cutting board for all to admire. If you are making this as part of a sandwich meal plan, carefully cut through the bread to divide it up into sandwich-size pieces, slicing horizontally and filling, then reassembling the focaccia artwork on a board or platter. Move over foot-longs, there's a new sandwich in town! Every bite is a beautiful and different flavor experience.

Focaccia bread is always best eaten warm out of the oven or within hours of being baked. Serve with various flavored oils, cheeses, dips, or spreads, and, of course, good wine. Focaccia bread art makes for a memorable dinner party, potluck, or as part of a grazing table at a wedding event. Have a destination party? Take a focaccia to your next tailgate party or gathering. Focaccia travels well when laid flat. I recommend using a large paper grocery bag, deli paper, or paper towels to wrap it in. You can use plastic; however, be aware that warm bread will sweat. Made with only grains, vegetables, herbs, fruits, seeds, and oils, these beautiful works of art are vegetarian- and/or vegan-friendly as well.

Leftovers, Storage, and Reheating

Focaccia bread is meant to be eaten fresh—warm out of the oven or within hours of baking it. You go through all the work of preparing a beautiful loaf of bread, so why wait to eat it. However, there are times when one must plan ahead. Here are my tips for storage and reheating for best results:

- Once the focaccia is completely cooled, use plastic wrap to double-wrap the bread. Be sure the whole bread is wrapped tightly.
- Breads can be frozen for a week or two, but no longer. Find a place in your freezer where the bread can lie flat, at least until it is fully frozen. Note: Breads tend to dehydrate and become brittle even after defrosting.
- To reheat, take the focaccia out of the freezer an hour prior to serving. Preheat the oven to 425°F (225°C; gas mark 7) with a baking sheet in it. Once the oven is up to temperature, carefully unwrap the focaccia, place it on the hot baking sheet, and allow it to heat for 6 to 8 minutes. It won't take long to reheat because of the olive oil on the outside of the dough. If you are outside at a cookout or tailgate party, after the meats have been grilled, turn the burner to low or move coals to the side, and place the focaccia directly on the grill. Allow to heat for 3 minutes, watching carefully—depending on the grill and heat, bread can burn rather quickly.

Essential Ingredients

Good homemade bread starts with good-quality ingredients and fresh everything—that includes flour, grains, and nuts. Always check dates on the flour. Same for nuts. All grains, nuts, and flours carry a certain number of oils, which can quickly go bad when sitting around in fluctuating temperatures. These are a few things I have on hand at all times, followed by a list of all the toppings used in the bread art recipes. Feel free to explore your own tastes and resources.

Butter: When a recipe calls for butter, it is always best to use unsalted. This keeps the salt amount completely in your control.

Cheese: While most bread art projects use produce for decorations, there are some that call for cheese. Semidry cheeses add the perfect accent of both color and flavor. Cheeses such as feta or dry, crumbled goat cheese create a desirable contrast of salty, tangy flavors that match perfectly with the sweetness of roasted vegetables.

Cinnamon: Ceylon cinnamon is the "true cinnamon," with a deep, rich taste. This cinnamon is native to Sri Lanka, formerly Ceylon, thus the name. This warm spice is derived from the *Cinnamomum zeylanicum* plant. Cassia cinnamon is the more common type found in grocery stores, but is not as flavorful as Ceylon.

Cocoa powder: Added to dough, cocoa powder creates a nice deep brown for contrast. Blended with a little oil into a thick paste, it can be painted on breads for stenciling and writing on doughs.

Dried fruits: Recipes that call for dried fruits are typically made with sweet focaccia. These are tender doughs baked at lower temperatures than regular focaccia breads. Because the fruits are dried, the sugars are more concentrated and can burn more easily. Soaking most dried fruits for 5 minutes in water gives a slight edge over the cooking process in the hot oven, resulting in dried fruits that are sweetly toasted.

Eggs: Use the freshest ones you can find. The words "free-range," "cage-free," "pasture-raised," "organic," and so on are relative terms and left to interpretation. Always look at the date on the package for freshness. Size and handling are also important. The average size for the smallest egg, the peewee is 1 ounce (28 g) all the way up to the jumbo at 3 ounces (85 g), and everything in between. This discrepancy can cause problems in a recipe. Most recipes use medium or large eggs.

Handling of eggs is important, too, with the greatest concern being salmonella. Refrigerated eggs need to stay refrigerated until ready to use. Recipes that call for room-temperature eggs should be taken out 1 to 2 hours prior to baking. If you forgot or they still feel cold, place them in warm water (not hot) for a few minutes. Room-temperature eggs whip up nicely because the proteins are loosened. Buy local eggs, if you can, for freshness.

Flour: Flours take center stage in all bread, as all the focaccia dough recipes in this book call for certain types of flour. Quality flour is essential to making good artisan bread. There are four main types for the recipes in this book—bread, all-purpose, whole wheat, and spelt. Try to avoid bleached flour. Wheat kernels are made up of layers of bran and a germ, along with endosperm, the center part that is processed into white flour. Unbleached and unbromated flours work best with bread recipes for overall flavor and quality of crust and crumb. Feel free to explore other flours as well.

Spelt flour is an ancient grain that is mentioned in certain recipes as an alternative to whole wheat flour. I love whole grain stone ground spelt. It is milder in flavor than regular hard winter wheat and slightly sweeter. If you want to try whole grains but don't care for the stronger flavor of regular whole wheat flour, spelt flour is a nice mild alternative. It has a slightly weaker gluten but still does a good job of bread making. The texture is wonderful too. I call it the well-behaved flour of baking—it is easy to work with and always does exactly what I want it to do.

In exciting flour news, flours by local grain growers and small millers are becoming more commonplace and no longer available just in grocery stores. A quick search on the internet for grain growers and millers may reveal some nearby options. Using locally grown grain supports farmers and millers, minimizes environmental impact, and gives baked bread an artisan quality and flavor above and beyond any you have ever tasted.

Herbs: Fresh herbs are used in most bread art projects. They are easy to access at any market or you could try keeping your own live plants—they are easy to grow and require minimal space and attention. Store-bought herbs will need some resuscitation. Best-care practices for all fresh herbs are to, as soon as you are able, place herbs in a bowl of ice water for about 15 minutes, then gently dry with a salad spinner or kitchen towel. This will revitalize them to their plump, green prepicked freshness. After reviving, place the stems in a jelly jar filled halfway with clean water, cover with a reusable plastic bag, and store in the refrigerator. Alternatively, after refreshing and drying, store in a reusable plastic bag with a paper napkin in the bag in the refrigerator. Some fresh herbs I recommend always having on hand in your crisper are basil, sage, and rosemary.

Before baking herbs on focaccia, it is important to soak them once again in a bowl of ice water to keep them plump and somewhat moist. Basil leaves stand a better chance of not turning brown in the oven if you place them on the dough slightly moist. Also try to avoid getting oil on basil while baking. Only use rosemary needles, never the woody stem. Thyme leaves are too tiny to hold up to the high heat for focaccia baking. I recommend adding them into the dough itself for a lovely flavor.

Nuts and seeds: Use raw unsalted nuts and seeds and roast them yourself as needed; this prevents them from being oversalted or expired. It is important to control the amount of salt in a baking recipe whether it be seeds, nuts, or butter, so it is best not to use the salted varieties. Another advantage to buying raw seeds and nuts is that they will not burn as fast in the oven. All nuts and seeds can be stored in the freezer in airtight containers until ready to use; this will help to preserve freshness.

Oil: I suggest using extra-virgin olive oil or a neutral oil in all my focaccia dough recipes. Topping my list is extra-virgin olive oil, as it imparts an earthy taste to any bread and has a high smoke point. If you don't care for the flavor that olive oil imparts, grapeseed oil has a beautiful color with a lovely mild flavor. It is a byproduct of winemaking, and who doesn't love upcycling, or wine, for that matter? Sunflower, safflower, vegetable, and refined coconut oils are good substitutes as well.

Pickled foods: Pickled peppers, cabbage, kale, onions, and all kinds of olives—small, large, mild, tangy, or salty—provide depth of flavor in each bite and preserve the bold colors of the vegetables when baked. Check out my easy recipes for Quick Pickled Vegetables (page 170).

Salt and finishing salt: Not too long ago there was just plain table salt and kosher salt. Now we can easily come across so many wonderful varieties and seasoned salts, which add exciting new flavors to baked goods and enhance and elevate our creations. I give options for using table salt and kosher salt in the focaccia dough recipes. I prefer using kosher salt because it is pure and has a clean taste. More specifically, I use Diamond Crystal Kosher Salt. The texture is light, allowing the crystals to blend into, melt, or stick to foods right away. Lighter crystals reduce the risk of oversalting as well. If you do use table salt for the recipes, follow the weight measurement in parentheses rather than volume, as table salt weighs significantly more than kosher salt. Always be in full control of your salt, which means not using any pre-salted products, such as butter, in a recipe.

In the world of bread baking, salt is added to bread recipes according to the total weight of the flour(s). A standard rule of thumb for salt in a bread recipe is for it to be 2 percent of the flour weight. For example, 35 ounces (1 kg) of flour would mean adding ¾ ounce (20 g) of salt. Salt plays several roles in good bread. It is a flavor enhancer, strengthens the gluten bonds, and slows down fermentation. Salt, once mixed with water, releases ions that inhibit yeast from fully absorbing water and natural sugars, thereby slowing down fermentation, which is a good thing. It's a fine balancing act between salt and the active cycle of yeast microbes in the mixing bowl that ultimately results in good bread.

Finishing salts are used as a topping rather than in the recipe itself. Fleur de sel, pink Himalayan, or true Hawaiian lava salt, which is salt that has been harvested from lava, are popular choices. Lava salt is salt that has been mixed with activated charcoal, adding a natural smoky flavor to foods. There are also some lovely herb-infused salts that can add much by way of flavor to focaccia bread art. My favorite finishing salts are crafted by Saltverk and harvested in the Westfjords of Iceland. They have a clean, light taste with a hint of umami. The crystals are light and flaky. For a more basic finishing salt, you can't go wrong with Maldon Sea Salt Flakes.

Sauces and creams: Basil Pesto (page 169) and Sun-Dried Tomato Pesto (page 169) are used in some of the bread art projects. I have provided a recipe for each, along with some other sauces; however, you can use store-bought sauces with a little doctoring of course. Store-bought varieties tend to be a bit oily. I would recommend buying fresh basil or sun-dried tomatoes and Parmesan to add in if you go that route. Clean and finely chop the basil or sun-dried tomatoes, then add them to the store-bought version, along with some Parmesan, and mix until you have a denser pesto. Use your discretion for amounts of these ingredients added: pesto should hold to a spoon when it is tipped upside down.

Sweet Lemon Cream (page 167) is used in sweet focaccia projects and has both dairy and egg as part of its ingredients. There are alternatives if those are a concern for you. Substitute egg for 1 tablespoon of ground flaxseed mixed with 1 tablespoon of water to make a flax egg, or use your favorite non-dairy cream cheese.

Vegetables: Fresh, firm, and colorful are keys to beautiful focaccia bread art. Fresh vegetables bake nicely in a hot oven. There are few exceptions to fresh, such as roasted red peppers and pickled purple cabbage. Some vegetables to keep in your crisper are a bag of colorful mini sweet peppers, red onions, scallions, garlic, leeks, colorful mini potatoes, zucchini, and grape and cherry tomatoes in a variety of colors. These veggies are found in most grocery stores and at farm stands and have other uses in meal applications. Shapes are just as important. For example, not all peppers have the same shape; when cut, some provide circles while others have enough ridges and valleys to resemble flowers. Choose according to your needs and chosen design. I once found a beautiful yellow pepper that had eight ridges and valleys. All I had to do was slice it and place it on a focaccia dough and, ta-da, flowers! Be picky about your produce—squeeze, poke, sniff, and scrutinize for the freshest and most colorful selection. I have been asked about using avocados. Stick to guacamole dip for your focaccia, as avocado turns bitter as it bakes.

Water: Hands down, when asked what one thing in baking you cannot do without, it would be water. For baking, room-temperature water works best, which is 70 to 72°F (21 to 22°C). For those using chlorinated water (tap water), fill mason jars and leave them on the counter, covered, for about an hour, or until ready to use. This helps dissipate the chlorine. Tap water works perfectly fine. In fact, rumor has it the tap water in New York City is what makes the famed NYC bagel so special.

Yeast: Instant, active dry, fresh brick, and rapid rise are familiar varieties available to home bakers. The recipes in this book all use instant yeast; however, you can use active dry or fresh (by weight) by simply taking a portion of the liquid from the recipe, adding either of these yeasts to the liquid, and allowing them to melt and bloom a bit before adding the rest of the liquid and flour(s). Do not use something called rapid, or quick, rise. Those are specifically for one-time rise recipes and do not work well for artisan bread recipes.

Essential Tools

Every artist has a box of tools they love to use for their craft. Baking—focaccia bread art to be more specific—is no different. Gathering a few of the essential tools will help make your projects a success. Nothing too fancy or outrageous is needed though. And most importantly, like an artist in an art studio, your kitchen comprises the artistic space and tools where many a beautiful dish is created, so give yourself comfort, organization, and space to create.

Baking sheets: Bakeries and restaurants use 18 x 13-inch (46 x 33 cm) heavy-gauge aluminum baking sheets or half-sheet pans for most of their oven work. These are now more readily available to home bakers. These heavy-gauge aluminum pans last forever, don't rust, stand up to high temperatures, bake evenly, and don't "pop," or warp, in the oven like more common household baking sheets. Make the investment in purchasing two of these pans and you will be set for life.

Bowl scraper: The third hand of the kitchen, this is a 6-inch (15 cm) white, flexible plastic scraper with a curved edge that fits perfectly in the groove of any bowl. You may already have one lurking in a kitchen drawer. They cost about a dollar; if you paid more, you paid too much. The bowl scraper can handle large scooping of scoopable stuff. It is a big help with mixing, as well as the gentle transfer of dough—it also safely works to get gunk off the counter without scratching (or frost off your windows without scratching). I do not recommend wooden spoons for the stirring or mixing process of breads; they are fibrous, which will cause dough to stick. Dough slides off plastic much more easily.

Bowls: Some of the recipes call for more than one bowl. I like to use restaurant-style stainless-steel bowls. They are easy to clean and stack inside each other for storing. Small and medium glass bowls can help when shaping.

Chopsticks: Say it with me, "May I have a set of chopsticks, please." Every time you get Chinese takeout, be sure to pick up your complimentary kitchen tools. Nothing fancy, just the wooden ones. Chopsticks make perfect utensils for stirring, poking, flipping, and eating, and take up little space, last forever, and are a quick wash. There is no need to coat chopsticks (or skewers, which also work well) with oil when using to help

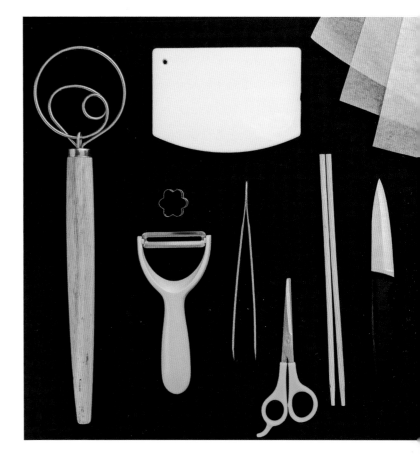

apply and secure decorations; however, some sticks are less smooth and it may be helpful to coat them with a bit of neutral oil to keep the dough and other foods from sticking.

Cookie and fondant cutters: These are available at most craft stores in the baking aisle and come in a variety of sizes. I find that the metal ones are the best for working with doughs and produce, although the plastic ones can work just as well with a bit more pressure. Be sure to keep them clean and dry.

Parchment paper: The unsung hero of the kitchen and easily the best little helper, parchment paper makes doing everything so much easier. It is nonstick, helps with gently moving dough, protects from burning, and helps remove bread from the pan seamlessly. I use it for every recipe and for most of my regular cooking too. Use it to make a template of your dough and set your vegetable design on it while prepping. Parchment makes transferring your dough and masterpieces easy, as well as the subsequent pan cleanup.

Silicone baking mats: These mats are nonstick, so they make cleanup easy. The downside is that they can hold flavors. Focaccia breads involve lots of neutral oil and savory ingredients, such as onions and garlic, which can permeate silicone mats. Your next batch of chocolate chip cookies could have a little unintended flavor! I tend to use them for baking sweet recipes and use parchment paper for all bread baking. I like Silpat brand.

Stand mixer (optional): This mixer is nice to have, but all recipes in this book can be made by hand. You do not need a stand mixer to accomplish high-quality artisan breads. I encourage you to make the doughs by hand to familiarize yourself with dough textures and changes that a dough goes through. As a matter of fact, many artisan bakers are returning to the old method of hand mixing for several reasons, including the risk of over-oxidation and overheating dough when using mixers. Over-oxidation depreciates the color and flavor of bread. Hand stretching allows the baker to know and have a good sense of the strength of the dough as it develops. The "new" old method of gentle stretching and folding (page 19) dough by hand allows for gluten to naturally develop its strength.

Spray bottle: A good tool for any kitchen is a clean spray bottle labeled for water use. This comes in handy for misting doughs that are drying out too fast or adding a little steam to the oven during the first 10 minutes of bread baking (though you don't need to do this for focaccia). It is also a handy way to keep cool on those hot summer days.

Whisk and Danish whisk: Whisks are used to thoroughly mix wet ingredients or aerate. A Danish whisk takes it a step further and really does a great job for mixing heavier ingredients such as dough.

Other Handy Tools

Scissors, tweezers, and a ruler that are for kitchen-use-only are great to have on hand. The scissors are great for cutting vegetables and pieces of dough, the tweezers help with precise placement of decorations, and the ruler assists in creating straight lines and exact measurements. A julienne peeler is also quite useful.

Essential Terms

Autolysis: This refers to the resting period for dough, which is usually 15 to 20 minutes, when the flour and water gets acquainted and creates a strong bond through hydration, which makes better textured and tasting bread. It can also refer to the stage in which the dough—more specifically the gluten— relaxes to make the work of shaping a bit easier.

Bulk fermentation: This is the term for the major rest time for dough after the first and second development stages, which allows dough to rest, covered in a warm, draft-free place, and double in volume. Yeast doughs on average take 1 to 2 hours.

Chiffonade cut: This is a special style of cut for fresh herb leaves, such as basil, and leafy greens. Stack 4 to 8 large leaves on top of each other, roll them into a cigar shape, and then run a knife through in narrow slices to create long strands.

Crumb: This is used to describe the interior texture of bread. For example, sourdough bread has a glossy large-holed crumb versus a tight crumb in a brioche, and then there is everything in between.

Degassing or Deflating: This is the act of deflating the dough after it has doubled in size. The gas is what makes the airy holes in the interior of the bread, which is a characteristic of good bread. For focaccia, degassing happens while you are shaping the dough onto the baking sheet.

Development: This happens when all the ingredients are incorporated along with air, friction, and time to create a smooth dough structure that is extensible, strong, and full of flavor.

Dimpling: Dimpling the dough is what focaccia is all about. It is a technique that gives focaccia a unique and delightful texture and is an easy technique to master. You simply sink your well-oiled fingers, all ten of them, down into a ripened dough on a baking sheet, very much like a piano player about to play a classical piece. Keep your fingers open wide, bent slightly, and use each finger to create dips and valleys in your dough, lifting and poking all around, intentionally controlling the shaping at the same time. It is such an enjoyable technique that some may go overboard. You may have the urge to start off with Mozart's *Sonata No. 11 in A Major (Alla Turca)* approach on your dough. This is too much, too fast. The best method is more like Beethoven's *Moonlight Sonata*. Slow and steady helps to stretch the dough so that it will comply better. This is an important step and the one that creates the best focaccia texture.

Docking: This is a method of reducing uneven baking and helps maintain a somewhat level bread. Focaccia is a delightfully bubbly, airy, crisp bread. The air bubbles are welcomed; however, some bubbles can be too big. Docking should only be done around some of the decorations with a skewer and/or toothpick to reduce the risk of them popping off during the bake. Docking should be minimal for focaccia dough and not done around the edges. Try to keep the holes about 3 inches (7.5 cm) apart.

Doubled or Doubling: It used to be that this was the standard measure for young doughs to spring to life. Older cookbooks mention allowing dough to double in size after the initial kneading and dough development, but times have changed and best practice is more like two-thirds of a rise from its original volume or just under doubled. Smell the dough; if it smells yeasty, sour, or pungent, that's a good sign its over-proofed. If using a glass bowl, mark it two-thirds of the way up from the top of the dough ball. If you are using a metal bowl, flatten the dough in the bottom, tear a tiny piece of dough off, and squish it about two-thirds of the way up on the wall of the bowl; when the dough mass hits that mark, it's ready. The goal is to achieve good flavor and leave enough of the dough's natural sugars for the final proofing stage—a fine balance indeed.

Dusting or Lightly floured: Knead or work the dough on a lightly floured surface—just enough flour to reduce sticking and friction. The best way to achieve lightly floured is to use a three-finger pinch of flour and then sidearm toss it in a quick motion, like the sidearm toss in Frisbee golf or a forehand in tennis. Throwing, tossing, or sprinkling directly overhead places too much flour on the work surface in some spots and can change the flavor and texture of dough. Have you ever tasted a spoon full of dry flour?

Enriched dough: Very different from lean dough (page 18), both in taste and texture, enriched dough is tender and delicate with a denser crumb. These doughs usually contain a fat, various flours, sweeteners, milk or dairy products, fruits, and nuts. Some good examples of enriched dough are brioche and raisin bread. For sweet doughs, because they are enriched, you will find the texture of the dough to be dense. This reduces the need for docking and should only be done for large air pockets if they occur. A gentle dimpling after you have shaped the dough will help create depth and texture. The key is not to over-dimple. Sweet dough needs gentle handling and time to rise undisturbed for that lovely airy texture like that of a donut.

Fall, Falling, or Fallen: This is when dough is over-risen and deflates. This can be a problem, as it is a sign of all the natural sugars being spent, or used up, in the process of fermentation (see below). If it appears to be falling, or deflating, deflate it all the way, reshape into a tight ball, cover, and pop it into the refrigerator. This will slow down the process.

Fermentation: This has become a popular method in the food world over the last few years. Natural fermentation in bread refers to the process by which the microbes in the yeast are essentially digesting the moistened flour, developing the flavor and texture that will become bread. Overnight fermentation takes bread to a whole new level of the most delightful flavor and texture. Without proper time for fermentation bread would taste like, well, Kleenex, to quote the famous French chef.

Kneading: This is the art of taking dough from the mixing bowl; laying it out on a flat surface; pushing, folding, and pulling the dough; and repeating until all is blended well and forms a ball. This method is used more commonly with enriched or multigrain doughs. Stretching and folding (page 19) tends to be a bit too challenging for multigrain, especially if rye flour is used. Rye has no gluten and rips easily, so it is best to mix in by kneading.

Lean dough or straight dough: This is dough that has very few ingredients, basically flour, water, salt, and yeast, or some variation of a natural starter. Good examples of lean dough are the classic French baguette and artisan country sourdough boule.

Lightly floured: See Dusting.

Oven spring: This is the initial "puffing up" of the bread dough during the bake in the oven, normally accomplished in the setting of high steam injected in high heat at the beginning of the bake. Some breads do not require this steaming, such as focaccia (though it won't hurt to steam it), but artisan breads are typically made in this fashion.

Over-ripening: See Fall, Falling, or Fallen

Proofing: This is the time allowed to let the dough rise and ferment after mixing and final shaping. The act of proofing, especially long proofing (fermentation), enhances the flavor and strength of dough. Regular proofing is done at room temperature, usually a minimum of 2 hours, or overnight proofing, which is normally done in the refrigerator for at least 6 hours or up to 24 hours. I love the overnight method for many reasons. The refrigerator method can be a great help if you want to prepare ahead and lighten the workload the next day. Not to mention the flavor and texture is superb. After the first rise at room temperature, which would be about 1 hour on the counter, simply oil a container or bowl with a lid large enough to leave room for expanding. Deflate the dough, make a tight ball, coat it lightly with a neutral oil, and place the dough in the refrigerator overnight. Take it out of the refrigerator the next day, 1 hour before starting your baking project. Give the dough a quick stretch and fold in the bowl, leaving it smooth side up, and let it rest. This method works with all the focaccia dough recipes in this book.

Rise: See Proofing.

Shaggy: This term describes a loose, somewhat lumpy texture of dough when it is initially mixed. The texture is wet but lumpy, like oatmeal, but slightly firmer. You may suspect you have a mess at first, but no fear; let it rest, come back in 15 minutes, and you will experience a whole new dough texture.

Shaping: This is the next step after the dough has finished proofing (page 18) and is just under-doubled (page 17) in size. For focaccia, there is little that needs to be done. After the dough is placed on a baking sheet, you simply use oiled and bent fingers—separated so that you look like you are about to play the piano, only you're playing to the dough—and push them down into the soft billowy dough to stretch it out to the desired shape. See dimpling (page 17) for more on this method. Loaf breads take a bit more skill. Round loaves are achieved through folding and friction. Folding a dough over itself four ways, then flipping it to the smooth side up. Cupping behind and pulling toward your torso will result in a tight ball, or boule, as they say in France. It takes a little practice, but everyone can achieve perfect loaves.

Slack dough: This is a dough that carries a lot of moisture and barely holds its shape when attempting to maintain a boule or quickly flattens back in the bowl after mixing.

Stretching and folding: This method replaces classic kneading (page 18) by using one hand to hold the rim of the bowl and the other hand for mixing. With wet fingers, grab the outer edge of the dough, pulling upward about 8 inches (20 cm) from the bowl or just before it tears, then fold over the body of the dough to the opposite side. The dough may want to tear on the first round of stretch and folds, and this is perfectly normal. You will feel a noticeable difference during the next ones as the gluten begins to develop. Two sets of stretching and folding are done during dough formation. A minimum of 10 to 12 stretch and folds for each set is all that is needed to make a well-developed, strong dough. To test the dough strength as you dive into the second set, after about four stretch and folds, attempt to pull the dough straight up and out of the bowl by one of the outer stretches. It will be so strong, you could bounce it.

Texture: This is referred to as the dough as it goes through the stages of development. It is also used to describe the interior and exterior of the bread once baked. Most desire a texture of a crisp crust and soft chewy interior.

Windowpane test: This is a method used to test the strength of a dough. You simply pull a piece of the dough upward from its mass and stretch it out using both hands. The dough should stretch nicely and form a thin film. If it doesn't, then the development needs to continue by more stretching and folding and/or kneading (page 18).

Bread Baking Tips

These are some general tips that I have gathered over my forty years of bread baking experience that I hope help you too. So, turn on some relaxing music to get you into your workflow and start baking!

Always read through the recipe. Before starting, read through the entire recipe, because it's no fun when you get to the part that says to refrigerate overnight when you were planning to serve the recipe that day.

Manage time. Yes, good bread takes time. It is one of the necessary ingredients of good bread. Plan accordingly. Become a multitasker and use proofing times to start gathering other ingredients for your focaccia project.

Find multitask tools. Speaking of multitasking, look around in the kitchen catch-all drawers for things that can work well for your bread projects. I use cannoli tubes once a year to make cannoli, but I use them over and over for bread projects. Skewers are not just for kebabs, but also for docking dough or poking decorations down into the dough. Find creative ways to use what you have. As I always say, "Think outside the bread box."

Gather ingredients. Measure out all the ingredients and have them set up in order of the ingedient list. This way, you will never miss an ingredient. The French have a name for this: mise en place (everything in place).

Follow ingredient order. Blending ingredients in a certain order is essential in cooking and baking, and bread is no exception. Placing yeast on top of flour can cause yeast clumps. Pouring salt over yeast will kill off yeast cells, rendering it inactive or weak. Lucky for us, most breads require minimal ingredients and steps. Premix any blended flours and dry ingredients in the bowl prior to adding liquids unless otherwise indicated in the recipe. Always make a well in the center of the flour mixture where liquids will then be added. Sprinkle yeast evenly across liquids as this ensures good distribution. Salt should be added last to yeasted breads (see page 13 to learn more about salt's role in bread making).

Oil the bowl. Always oil the bowl on the final rise and your dough will happily slide right out.

Find a warm place for dough to rise. Well, it goes without saying that when you start baking bread in your kitchen, it will express the very essence of warmth. However, sometimes our homes are just a bit too cool for bread making. Here are a few tips on where you can find warm environments in your kitchen: on top of the refrigerator, on the counter area where the dishwasher is being run, on the stove top, or on an espresso machine with a tank. An inexpensive proofing method is to take one of those large plastic storage bins, flip it upside down on the counter with the bowl of dough covered underneath, add 2 cups (480 ml) of hot water and, voilà, a professional proofer (sort of). You also want to make sure your proofing spot is draft-free.

Clean flour spills. You're going to do it eventually—spill flour that is. After sweeping up what you can, there is always a little bit left. Try wetting the bristles of your dustpan broom before the final sweeps. It works every time, and then just rinse the bristles before putting the broom away.

Wet fingers. If you wet your fingers before stretching or handling your dough, the dough will not stick to your hands. This trick works at any stage of a recipe.

Understand your oven. Every oven is different. How your bread bakes is based on the correct temperature and where the rack is in the oven. Always use the middle rack. If you have a baking stone, feel free to use. Stones retain good heat, but you may have to adjust the temperature and time. I recommend getting an inexpensive temperature gauge to hang in the oven so you can know if your oven knobs are telling you the truth or not. Artisan bread bakes at a high temperature at the beginning, to give them oven spring (page 18). The temperature is then turned down to complete the browning.

Prevent burning. The number-one question I get asked is how to stop bread art decorations from burning. There are a few careful measures you can take, but the key is moisture content. The more moisture a garnish has, the less likely it is to burn. For herbs, always keep them soaking in a bowl of ice water until you are ready to use them. A teaspoon of fresh lemon juice helps to keep them green as well. Lay them on the dough and then sprinkle just a bit of water on the leaves themselves, being careful not to get them too wet, just moist. For nuts, use unsalted raw nuts as they will be getting toasted during the baking process. Sun-dried tomatoes and other dried fruits, such as raisins and dates, stand a better chance if they are rehydrated slightly as well. Place both nuts and dried fruits in warm water for 5 to 10 minutes and pat dry just before using. Fresh produce has little chance of burning during the short baking time; however, this depends on the oven you are using. Some have hotter temps from the top down, which can cause issues. A simple solution is to make a foil tent: place a loose piece of tented foil over the top, but don't secure it to the pan at all; this will divert the intensity of the heat away from the toppings. Foil tents are a nuisance if you are using a convection oven, though. It just becomes a kite in the oven. I don't recommend using a convection oven for artisan bread baking, especially flatbreads, but if you are using one, turn off the convection, if possible, when using a foil tent.

Write things down. The kitchen is where new discoveries are made. When you're baking, have a notebook with a pen nearby for writing notes, sketches, or recipe corrections. I always have a small notebook in the kitchen while baking or cooking. Make notes about your oven's behaviors or any adjustments you made to a recipe to make it yours. The kitchen is a science lab—sometimes you come across a happy accident, something you did that worked even though it was not in the original recipe. If I am working from a cookbook, I will jot notes right in the cookbook. Be sure to note the date of the recipe you are working on to help with future reference. Measurements, time, and temperature are all important to keep track of as well.

Making the Cut

Here's a quick rundown of how to prep and transform some of the more commonly used vegetables and herbs into bread art decorations. Feel free to be a produce explorer and try new flavors and colors offered at markets and farm stands. Vegetables can be prepped 12 hours ahead and stored in airtight containers with lids in the refrigerator.

Beets

There are no easy solutions for the so-called bleeding of beets. The color runs deep; however, here is a tip for using them on focaccia: after you have cut the desired shapes from the beet, drop them in a pot of just boiled water with a little lemon juice for 10 minutes, then lay on a paper towel to dry. This will take away most of the staining.

Garlic

Pre-peeled garlic is not fresh garlic. When you choose a bulb of garlic, be sure to squeeze it; it should not have any give whatsoever. A tight bulb is a fresh bulb. The easiest way to peel garlic is to separate the cloves, stick them in a small glass jar with a lid, and shake vigorously. This friction loosens the papery outer skins—an easy and fun method. Slice garlic either lengthwise or crosswise to provide intense savory flavor and color to focaccia. After baking, the result should be a nice brown color.

Herbs

Basil, parsley, arugula, chives, sage, and rosemary are all wonderful additions to bread art and enrich the flavor as well as add color. The key to baking with herbs is to keep them fresh. Always place prepped herbs in a bowl of ice water with a teaspoon of lemon juice to keep their color bright. Most herbs do not have to be cut, but the woody stems do need to be removed. Rosemary and sage are the woodiest. Use only the needles of rosemary, keeping to 2 or 3 needles per placement so as not to overwhelm the bread. Sage also has a strong flavor, so don't use too much on your bread.

SOAKING VEGETABLES AND HERBS IN ICE WATER

Soaking vegetables and herbs gives them the upper hand in a hot oven. It keeps the colors vibrant and tightens the membranes of the vegetables while plumping up herbs. After fraying pepper rings, shallots or onions (making cuts in one end and spreading out to make a fringe effect), soak them in ice water for about an hour, and you will find beautiful "bloomed" flowers ready for your focaccia dough.

Leeks

Leeks are my favorite allium. They are sturdy and hold up to high heat. Their layers can be cut into many shapes and provide a spectrum of greens, from yellowish to deep-forest green. They bake into a delicious sweet-savory flavor. The only gripe I have is that they really are quite sandy and need to be washed well. Slice off ¼ inch (6 mm) from the bottom of the leek. Make a shallow, lengthwise slit down one side of the leek, then peel off and discard the outer layer, which is usually dry and damaged. Carefully separate the remaining layers and wash each piece under cold running water to remove dirt and sand.

Calla lily flower: Take a leek layer and gently fold it in half, starting at the palest (white) end. Using kitchen scissors, cut a rounded diamond shape that narrows at the top and bottom of the white part. As you approach the green part, use the scissors to make a long, narrow cut to create a stem about ½ inch (1 cm) wide and 4 to 6 inches (10 to 15 cm) long. The whole flower, including the stem, should be 6 to 8 inches (15 to 20 cm) in length. When opened back up, you should have a lovely calla lily.

Mini Sweet Peppers (and Bell Peppers)

These peppers normally come in a bag with three colors—red, yellow, and orange—and approximately a dozen or so to a bag. I always try to find bags with equal amounts of colors and shapes. There are round ones, tiny ones, and flat oval-shaped ones. A little extra effort can provide a lot of options for decorations. These flavor-packed peppers are easy to clean with minimal seeds, and their thinner flesh makes them flexible for cutting.

Thin flower petals, straight cut: Trim 1 inch (2.5 cm) from the bottom and top of the pepper, reserving the trimmings for other applications. Slice the pepper in half lengthwise and remove and discard seeds and pith. Flatten one half, smooth side down, and slice lengthwise into thin strips. To make matchstick-size pieces, cut the longer strips into shorter pieces. Keep the different colored strips separate until ready to decorate.

Thin flower petals, round cut: Choose a rounder-shaped pepper. Trim 1 inch (2.5 cm) from the bottom and top of the pepper, reserving the trimmings for other applications. Cut the pepper into crosswise rings about ¼ inch (6 mm) wide, removing and discarding seeds and pith.

Splayed flower, frayed cut: Carefully remove the stem and seeds from the pepper top, reserving the body for another use. Lay the pepper top on its side and make slits inside, about ⅛ inch (3 mm) apart. Place in ice water, and the pepper will open like a flower.

Oval flower petals: Use a mini pepper with a flat oval shape. Slice into half ovals; it will yield 6 to 8 ovals in various sizes. When placed lengthwise, they become oblong circles perfect for a caterpillar body!

Cutting shapes with cookie cutters: Trim 1 inch (2.5 cm) from the bottom and top of the pepper, reserving the trimmings for other applications. Slice the pepper in half lengthwise and remove and discard seeds and pith. Flatten one half, smooth side down. Press the cutter into the interior part of the pepper, applying pressure and giving a bit of a twisting motion to be sure the cutter goes through the skin of the pepper.

Mushrooms

Mushrooms contain anywhere from 85 to 95 percent water. To use them, sauté them prior to decorating your bread to reduce the amount of water in them. Mushrooms bring delicious earthy flavors and umami to any dish.

Olives

Pitted black and kalamata olives and green olives, pitted or stuffed with pimiento, bake well and add a nice flavor to any bread art, as well as being versatile in their use as decorations. Always pat the olives dry and slice either in half crosswise or in thinner slices crosswise, depending on what the design calls for.

Onions

It is easy to find a variety of colors and shapes in these flavor-packed alliums. The red onion is a popular choice not only because of its color but it also offers premade flowers just through slicing. When shopping for onions, know your intended use. If it's a long-stem-flower project, look for long oval onions; for cutouts and shapes, I suggest using larger round onions that barely fit in your hand. These have layers of colors and provide ample surface space for cookie cutters.

Fanned out: Remove only the outer layer of dry skin. Slice the onion down the middle lengthwise, keeping the bottom root part intact. Make ¼-inch (6 mm) slices lengthwise. These can be trimmed off the top to reveal a semi-opened chrysanthemum-like flower. Or leave the top intact and cut the bottom to reveal large open petals, which can be used plain or filled with more color.

Small, unopened flower buds: After slicing a red onion in half lengthwise, you will notice little oblong shapes that come to a point in the middle of the onion. Carefully remove them for lovely unopened flower buds.

Cutting shapes with a knife: Using a paring knife, cut a pointed petal shape through 3 or 4 layers to give different sizes and shapes. Use cookie cutters for little flower shapes in purple, or flip them over for a brilliant pale purple-white color.

Cutting shapes with cookie cutters: Cut the onion in half lengthwise, root side to bottom. Set one half aside and lay the other half flat side down. Cut in half vertically from top to root, then separate out 3 or 4 layers, keeping them together. This makes it easier to cut through with the cookie cutter. If it appears to be too hard to cut through, try flipping the onion over and attempting to push the cutter through the interior side.

Potatoes

Mini colorful potatoes are delicious, bake well, and are great for cutting out shapes with cookie cutters. To cut out shapes, trim down one side of the potato to create a flat surface, then lay the flat side down and begin cutting out shapes. If the potato is too large to get the cutter through, trim the potato to accommodate the depth and size of the cutter.

Roasted Red Peppers

Roasted red peppers add a nice smoky flavor and vibrant red color to focaccia bread art. Though you can buy jarred and canned peppers, it's very easy to roast red peppers yourself. Before placing a strip of roasted red pepper on the dough, pat it dry to remove excess moisture.

Scallions

Scallions are mainly used for straight lines, stems, and curling vines. Select the greenest ones you can

HOW TO ROAST RED PEPPERS

Purchase several fresh dark-red sweet peppers, the darker the red, the more flavor. Wash, dry, and rub the red peppers with olive oil. Place them in a shallow baking tray and place under a hot broiler. Let the outer skins get blistery and dark, almost burnt. Rotate onto each side until each side has turned blistery and brown. Remove from the broiler and place immediately into a small paper lunch bag or in a sealed container. Allow to cool completely. The peppers will become quite soft. Working over a bowl, pull out the green stem. Use caution here as there will be lots of juice that pours out. You can reserve some of the juice for storing peppers in. Remove and discard the seeds. Remove the burnt skins by simply peeling away the outer layer. The skin should come off easily. Leave the peppers whole and place them in a jar. Pour some of the reserved liquid in the jar, cover tightly, and store in the refrigerator. If you don't plan to use right away, you can freeze them in airtight containers. Although most would add a bit of salt at this point before storing, I do not. I salt to taste according to what I am using the red peppers for instead.

find. Keeping scallions healthy and plump is key to freshness. Ice water helps to revive scallions that have been sitting on the shelf in the market.

Flower stems: Cutting along the bias of a scallion, or lengthwise, is the most common cut. Cut off the bottom, about a ½ inch (1 cm). Slice each green portion in half. If they are rather thick, you can make another cut. They should be about a ½ inch (1 cm) wide. There is sometimes a small, solid sprout in the center. These should be left whole; they are usually curved and give depth to bread art.

Curly vines: Slice the green portion of the scallion into thin strips about ⅛ inch (3 mm) wide and place in ice water for at least 15 to 20 minutes—they will curl up nicely.

Small circles: Scallions provide lovely centers for flowers or just a nice white circle. Simply cut the scallions crosswise into ¼-inch-thick (6 mm) slices.

Sun-Dried Tomatoes

Because sun-dried tomatoes are so dense with natural sugars, be sure to soak them for 10 minutes in room-temperature water so that they will not burn as a topping on your bread. Lay soaked tomatoes on a paper towel to absorb excess water.

Tomatoes

The smaller the tomato the more flavor, so I prefer to use grape or cherry tomatoes that come in a package with a variety of colors. The longer tomatoes bake, the sweeter they become. There are many uses for tomatoes in focaccia garden art. My very favorite is clustered together to represent grapes or hanging flower buds. Always place sliced tomatoes on a paper towel or cotton kitchen towel after slicing. This absorbs excess moisture and some of the seeds. Wet vegetables lead to soggy bread, which has an unpleasant texture or mouthfeel and can be easily avoided. A tiny sprinkle of salt on the cut sides brings out more of the tomato flavor.

Measuring Focaccia Dough Ingredients

When making the focaccia dough recipes starting on page 29, it is important that you measure the ingredients as exact as possible for best results. I recommend using the metric measurements in parentheses and weighing your ingredients on a digital food scale. If you don't have a digital food scale, you can still use your standard measuring cups, tablespoons, and teaspoons; just make sure when measuring flour, especially, that you dip the measuring cup and/or spoon into the flour bag or cannister and level it off from there. You also want your salt and yeast measurements to be level. Regarding water temperature, have a thermometer at hand to make sure the water is at the temperature noted in the recipe.

Latticework, Braiding & Stenciling

These are some techniques for focaccia dough that can add even more visual interest to your bread art projects.

Latticework

Contrasting dough colors can bring more depth and interest to your focaccia. A heavy-duty lattice cutter can be a big help to create this decorative second layer of color. If you don't have a lattice cutter, no worries; you can also achieve a great lattice by hand. Here's how to create a lattice using both methods.

Using a Lattice Tool

1. On a lightly floured surface, place the portion of dough as directed in the project. Using a rolling pin, roll out the dough into an 11 x 8-inch (28 x 20 cm) rectangle that is ¼ inch (6 mm) thick. Lightly flour the top of the dough too.

2. Holding the lattice tool on the 8-inch (20 cm) side of the dough, with one sweeping motion while applying pressure with the tool, move the tool across the dough from one end to the other. Repeat with the next sections, leaving a ¼-inch (6 mm) space in between each line you cut.

3. Just prior to applying the lattice to your base dough, brush the base dough with egg wash (1 egg mixed with ¼ cup, or 60 ml, water) or just plain water, then gently lift the lattice dough and lay it across the base dough, spreading the lattice dough strands apart and creating little squares or diamond shapes. Tuck any overhanging pieces underneath the focaccia.

4. Decorate each square or diamond with a variety of colors using vegetables, seeds, nuts, herbs, or fruits.

5. Bake as directed.

Creating a Lattice by Hand

1. On a lightly floured surface, place the portion of dough as directed in the project. Using a rolling pin, roll out the dough into an 11 x 8-inch (28 x 20 cm) rectangle that is ¼ inch (6 mm) thick. Lightly flour the top of the dough too. Using a ruler and a paring knife or pizza cutter, cut long strips that are ¼ inch (6 mm) wide. Separate each strip so that they don't stick together, using enough flour to help prevent sticking.

2. Starting at the bottom corner of the focaccia dough, lay the strips parallel to each other diagonally and evenly spaced. You will need to trim some of the strips as you go along, leaving enough to tuck underneath the focaccia dough. Use the longest strips for the middle and shorter ones toward the edges.

3. Starting at the edge closest to you, fold back the second and fourth strips toward you, lay a shorter strip of dough perpendicular to other dough strips, then trim, leaving enough dough to tuck under the focaccia dough. Fold the second and fourth strips back down over the strip, but do not tuck it in yet.

4. Fold back the first, and every other strip toward you, then lay another strip of dough across the focaccia dough. Unfold the first, third, and fifth strips over the new strip. Repeat these steps until the focaccia lattice design is complete.

5. Secure the loose ends of the lattice by tucking the dough strips underneath the focaccia dough. Using a pastry brush, coat the area using either egg wash (1 egg mixed with ¼ cup, or 60 ml, water) or just plain water to help the lattice to adhere to the focaccia dough.

6. Decorate each square with a variety of colors using vegetables, seeds, nuts, herbs, or fruits.

7. Bake as directed.

Braiding

If you know how to braid rope or hair, then braiding dough should be a piece of cake, or in this case, a piece of bread. Here's how to create a three-strand braid with dough.

1. Lay 3 equal-size strands of dough vertically alongside each other. Pinch the tops together, then slightly separate the strands.

2. Beginning with the right strand, bring it across the middle strand, overlapping it and laying it at the left side of the middle strand. Take the left strand and bring it across the middle strand, laying it at its right side. Repeat, bringing the right strand back over the middle, making sure to keep them snug at the top as you go along. Repeat until you have a completed braid, then pinch the ends together.

Stenciling

Stencil patterns have become popular in the food world, especially in bread baking. You can use any pliable stencils found at craft stores and home improvement centers. With a variety of edible colors such as cocoa powder, rice flour, spices, and vegetable powders to enhance your bread art, it's all about finding a pattern you like. To stencil dough, always wet the surface of the dough either by spritzing it with water or brushing it with honey glue (equal parts honey mixed with water). If you would like a color resulting in a deeper brown, you can use oil. Just before the dough is ready to go into the oven, gently hold the stencil in place on the dough, being careful not to deflate, and using a soft-bristle, food-safe brush, dust the powder over the stencil in small dabs. Carefully wipe away any excess powder before lifting the stencil off the dough. Bake as directed.

Focaccia Dough Recipes

These doughs are versatile and can be shaped to accommodate many styles of bread. They are all yeasted doughs that take approximately two hours to develop, or they can be stored in the refrigerator overnight for longer proofing and fermentation. Though certain recipes are recommended for each project, you can use any of the recipes, unless otherwise indicated. Each recipe in this section makes one large focaccia to fit an 18 x 13-inch (46 x 33 cm) pan, which is most common for the projects in this book, or four mini breads or eight 3-ounce (85 g) buns.

Basic White Focaccia

This straightforward yeasted dough is most commonly used for focaccia bread. The texture is chewy and airy inside with a deep-brown golden crust. This recipe is a perfect place to start if you have never made yeasted breads before.

YIELD: 1 FOCACCIA

2 teaspoons (12 g) table salt or 1 tablespoon plus 1 teaspoon (12 g) kosher salt

6 tablespoons plus 2 teaspoons extra-virgin olive or neutral oil, divided (3 tablespoons for dough, 2 teaspoons for oiling the bowl, and 3 tablespoons for oiling the baking sheet and coating the dough)

4½ cups (640 g) bread flour

2 cups (450 ml) room-temperature water (70 to 72°F, or 21 to 22°C)

1 packet or 2¼ teaspoons (7 g) instant yeast

Finishing salt, to taste (optional)

Initial Mixing

1. Measure out the salt and 3 tablespoons of the oil and set aside.

2. Place the flour in a large bowl. Make a well in the middle of the flour, then add the room-temperature water to the well. Sprinkle the yeast over the liquid.

3. Using a bowl scraper, blend the flour with the water and yeast by moving around the bowl from the outside and bringing the flour to the middle. Use a chopping motion to initially mix the flour into the water-yeast mixture.

4. When most of the flour has been absorbed, use your hands to finish incorporating all the flour until a shaggy ball (page 19) forms. Once all the flour has been incorporated and there is no dry flour left, cover the dough and let rest in a warm, draft-free place for 15 minutes. This step is known as autolysis (page 16).

Multitask Moment

While the dough is resting, start gathering the other ingredients for your chosen project.

Dough Development and First Rise

1. Uncover the dough in the bowl. Sprinkle the pre-measured salt over the top of the dough and drizzle the pre-measured oil around the circumference of the dough.

2. With wet fingers, squish the salt and oil into the dough.

3. Once all the ingredients are well blended, begin the first set of stretch and folds (page 19), 10 to 12 times.

4. Cover the dough and let rest in a warm, draft-free place for an additional 15 to 20 minutes.

Dough Development and Second Rise

1. Uncover the rested dough and repeat 10 to 12 stretch and folds.

2. Coat the bowl with 2 teaspoons of the oil, add the dough, and cover. (If you need to start the recipe ahead of time, at this point the dough can be stored in an airtight container in the refrigerator for up to 48 hours.)

3. Allow the dough to proof, covered, in a warm, draft-free place for about 1 hour. The dough should just about double in size and be smooth and supple.

Multitask Moment

Begin to prepare the decorations for your chosen project.

Oven Preparation

Thirty minutes prior to baking, move the oven rack to the middle and preheat the oven to 450°F (230°C; gas mark 8), allowing time for the oven to come to full temperature. If you are using a baking stone, preheat the oven for at least 45 minutes to allow for the oven and stone to come to full temperature.

Shaping

1. Line an 18 x 13-inch (46 x 33 cm) baking sheet with parchment paper and oil it with 1 tablespoon of the oil.

2. Using a bowl scraper or oiled hand, gently transfer the dough to the middle of the sheet with the smooth side of the dough facing up. If the dough lands upside down, gently flip it over so that the smooth side is up.

3. Gently begin shaping and dimpling (page 17) the dough using all ten fingers, piano style, to press down into the dough. Shape the dough into a rectangular dough "canvas," about 16 x 11 inches (41 x 28 cm), leaving space on all sides for expansion. If the dough is springing back, allow it to rest for 5 to 8 minutes. After this rest, the dough will be supple and ready for shaping again.

Decorating

1. Coat the dough with the remaining 2 tablespoons oil, then decorate the focaccia according to the directions of your chosen project.

2. Once you have finished decorating, survey the surface and deflate any large air bubbles with a toothpick or skewer, leaving smaller ones intact. Give a few pokes all around the dough to level out the playing field, so to speak—this is called docking (page 17). Using piano-style finger motions, gently dimple the dough again. Ultimately, you want to see an uneven bubbly texture, about 1½ to 2 inches (4 to 5 cm) thick in various spots. If the focaccia is flat, allow it to rest for 8 to 10 minutes in a warm, draft-free place.

Baking

1. Just before placing the focaccia in the oven, check the decorations to be sure they are all snug. Secure any that look to be popping off using a chopstick, skewer, or your fingers.

2. Add finishing salt (if using) and place the focaccia on the middle rack.

3. Bake for 8 minutes at 450°F (230°C; gas mark 8), then reduce the heat to 375°F (190°C; gas mark 5) and check the decorations again. If any are popping off, coerce them back into the dough by gently and carefully poking down. You don't want to burn yourself or deflate the dough. Bake for 10 to 16 more minutes, until the focaccia is golden brown and crisp on the edges.

4. It can be extremely tempting to cut into a nice hot loaf of bread straight out of the oven, but it is important to allow the bread to cool slightly and let off a little steam, so to speak, because the bread is still finishing its bake after being removed from the oven. Let rest for 5 to 10 minutes before cutting.

Baking with a Baking Stone

If using a baking stone, slide the focaccia onto a peel using the parchment paper for easy transfer. Place the focaccia directly onto the stone with the parchment underneath and bake for 18 to 22 minutes, depending on the masonry you are using and its thickness. Check the bottom of the focaccia after 10 minutes of baking, reducing the temperature to 375°F (190°C; gas mark 5). If it appears to be getting too dark, move it back to the pan and finish baking it in the pan until the top is golden brown.

FLAVOR VARIATIONS

Kalamata olive, rosemary, and poppy seed: Add ⅓ cup (50 g) of chopped pitted kalamata olives, 1 tablespoon of chopped fresh rosemary, and 1 tablespoon of poppy seeds to the dough with the salt and oil in step 1 of the Dough Development and First Rise stage. Blend well.

Leek and sage: Clean and slice 1 medium leek into ½-inch (1 cm) rings and mince enough fresh sage until you have 1 tablespoon. Coat a medium skillet with 2 teaspoons of olive oil. Add the leek and sage to the pan with a dash of salt and cook and stir over medium heat for 7 to 8 minutes, until the leeks are tender. Some light browning on the edges may occur, which is okay. Add the cooked leek and sage to the dough with the salt and oil in step 1 of the Dough Development and First Rise stage. Blend well.

Basic Whole Wheat Focaccia

The whole wheat flour adds a denser interior to this bread and a slightly softer crust with an earthy, sweet roasted flavor. If you would like a milder whole wheat flavor, look for whole-grain spelt or try finding locally sourced freshly milled whole wheat flour. Both are on the nuttier side in flavor and fresher than store-bought.

YIELD: 1 FOCACCIA

2 teaspoons (12 g) table salt or 1 tablespoon plus 1 teaspoon (12 g) kosher salt

6 tablespoons plus 2 teaspoons extra-virgin olive or neutral oil, divided (3 tablespoons for dough, 2 teaspoons for oiling the bowl, and 3 tablespoons for oiling the baking sheet and coating the dough)

3 cups (445 g) bread flour

1¼ cups (185 g) whole wheat flour or whole grain spelt flour

2 cups (450 ml) room-temperature water (70 to 72°F, or 21 to 22°C) you may need to add 2 or 3 more tablespoons of room-temperature water, 1 tablespoon at a time, until you have the texture of a very soft and supple dough that stretches and folds easily yet keeps its shape depending on the type of whole wheat flour you use)

1 packet or 2¼ teaspoons (7 g) instant yeast

Finishing salt, to taste (optional)

Initial Mixing

1. Measure out the salt and 3 tablespoons of the oil and set aside.

2. Blend the flours together in a large bowl. Make a well in the middle of the flour, then add the water to the well. Sprinkle yeast over the liquid.

3. Using a bowl scraper, blend the flour with the room-temperature water by moving around the bowl from the outside and bringing flour to the middle. Use a chopping motion to initially mix the flour into the water-yeast mixture.

4. When most of the flour has been absorbed, use your hands to finish incorporating all the flour until a shaggy ball (page 19) forms. Once all the flour has been incorporated and there is no dry flour left, cover the dough and let rest in a warm, draft-free place for 15 minutes. This step is known as autolysis (page 16).

Multitask Moment

While the dough is resting, start gathering the other ingredients for your chosen project.

Dough Development and First Rise

1. Uncover the dough in the bowl. Sprinkle the pre-measured salt over the top of the dough and drizzle the pre-measured oil around the circumference of the dough.

2. With wet fingers, squish the salt and olive oil into the dough.

3. Once all the ingredients are well blended, begin the first set of stretch and folds (page 19), 10 to 12 times.

4. Cover the dough and let rest in a warm, draft-free place for an additional 15 to 20 minutes.

Dough Development and Second Rise

1. Uncover the rested dough and repeat 10 to 12 stretch and folds.

2. Coat the bowl with 2 teaspoons of the oil, add the dough, and cover. (If you need to start the recipe ahead of time, at this point the dough can be stored in an airtight container in the refrigerator for up to 48 hours.)

3. Allow the dough to proof, covered, in a warm, draft-free place for about 1 hour. The dough should just about double in size and be smooth and supple.

Multitask Moment

Begin to prepare the decorations for your chosen project.

Oven Preparation

Thirty minutes prior to baking, move the oven rack to the middle and preheat the oven to 450°F (230°C; gas mark 8), allowing time for the oven to come to full temperature. If you are using a baking stone, preheat the oven for at least 45 minutes to allow for the oven and stone to come to full temperature.

Shaping

1. Line an 18 x 13-inch (46 x 33 cm) baking sheet with parchment paper and oil it with 1 tablespoon of the oil.

2. Using a bowl scraper or oiled hand, gently transfer your dough to the middle of the sheet with the smooth side of the dough up. If the dough lands upside down, gently flip it over so that the smooth side is up.

3. Gently begin shaping and dimpling (page 17) the dough using all ten fingers, piano style, to press down into the dough. Shape the dough into a rectangular dough "canvas," about 16 x 11 inches (41 x 28 cm), leaving space on all sides for expansion. If the dough is springing back, allow it to rest for 5 to 8 minutes. After this rest, the dough will be supple and ready for shaping again.

Decorating

1.   Coat the dough with the remaining 2 tablespoons oil, then decorate the focaccia according to the directions of your chosen project.

2.   Once you have finished decorating, survey the surface and deflate any large air bubbles with a toothpick or skewer, leaving smaller ones intact. Give a few pokes all around the dough to level out the playing field, so to speak—this is called docking (page 17). Using piano-style finger motions, gently dimple the dough again. Ultimately, you want to see an uneven bubbly texture, about 1½ to 2 inches (4 to 5 cm) thick in various spots. If the focaccia is flat, allow it to rest for 8 to 10 minutes in a warm, draft-free place.

Baking

1.   Just before placing the focaccia in the oven, check the decorations to be sure they are all snug. Secure any that look to be popping off, using a chopstick, skewer, or your fingers.

2.   Add finishing salt (if using) and place the focaccia on the middle rack.

3.   Bake for 8 minutes at 450°F (230°C; gas mark 8), then reduce the heat to 375°F (190°C; gas mark 5) and check the decorations again. If any are popping off, coerce them back into the dough by gently and carefully poking down. You don't want to burn yourself or deflate the dough. Bake for 10 to 16 more minutes, until the focaccia is golden brown and crisp on the edges.

4.   It can be extremely tempting to cut into a nice hot loaf of bread straight out of the oven, but it is important to allow the bread to cool slightly and let off a little steam, so to speak, because the bread is still finishing its bake after being removed from the oven. Let rest for 5 to 10 minutes before cutting.

Baking with a Baking Stone

If using a baking stone, slide the focaccia onto a peel using the parchment paper for easy transfer. Place the focaccia directly onto the stone with the parchment underneath and bake for 18 to 22 minutes, depending on the masonry you are using and its thickness. Check the bottom of the focaccia after 10 minutes of baking, reducing the temperature to 375°F (190°C; gas mark 5). If it appears to be getting too dark, move it back to the pan and finish baking it in the pan until the top is golden brown.

PRE-FERMENT METHOD

Once you have tried the basic straight dough method, up your bread game and try a pre-ferment version. This method is used widely in French bakeries, made popular by Raymond Calvel, who was the pioneer of artisan breads. Pre-ferment is sometimes called a poolish. This method is a way to elevate texture and flavor, creating a soft airy interior, a strong crust, a warm-sweet fragrance, and deep aromatic toasted grain notes. Poolish or pre-ferment is made by mixing water, flour, and the tiniest bit of yeast together. If you don't have time to attend to the dough the next day, don't worry; pre-ferment/ poolish is good for 3 days in the refrigerator.

For Basic White Focaccia: The night before you plan to bake use 1 cup (148 g) of the flour and ¾ cup (168 ml) of the water along with ½ teaspoon of the instant yeast from the main recipe (page 30). Place this in a bowl and mix to combine. Cover tightly and store in the refrigerator overnight. The next day, add the remaining water and yeast and mix until well combined. Add the remaining flour and mix to a shaggy ball (page 19). Cover and let rest for 15 minutes in a warm, draft-free place then proceed with the rest of the instructions.

For Basic Whole Wheat Focaccia: Measure out and mix both the flours together. Extract 1 cup (148 g) of the flour mixture, ¾ cup (168 ml) of the water, and ½ teaspoon of the instant yeast from the main recipe (see above). Place these ingredients in a large bowl and mix to combine. Cover tightly and store in the refrigerator overnight. The next day, add the remaining water and yeast, and mix until well combined. Add the remaining flour mixture and mix to a shaggy ball (page 19). Cover and let rest for 15 minutes in a warm, draft-free place, then proceed with the rest of the instructions.

Dark Multigrain Focaccia

Though this is a thick, dense whole-grain bread that has a tight crumb and softer crust, it makes up for it with its rich grain flavors. This dough does better with traditional hand kneading on a counter or table, but you can also use a stand mixer if you have one.

YIELD: 1 FOCACCIA

2½ cups (362 g) bread flour, plus more for dusting

½ cup (74 g) whole wheat flour

¼ cup (38 g) buckwheat or spelt flour

¼ cup (38 g) rye flour

¼ cup (30 g) wheat bran

¼ cup (25 g) quick oats

¼ cup (40 g) coarse cornmeal

1½ tablespoon dark cocoa powder

2 teaspoons (12 g) table salt or salt or 1 tablespoon plus 1 teaspoon (12 g) kosher salt

2 tablespoons seeds of your choice (such as millet, poppy, sesame, sunflower, flax, etc.)

1½ packets or 3⅜ teaspoons (11 g) instant yeast

1½ cups (340 ml) room-temperature water (70 to 72°F, or 21 to 22°C)

¼ cup (65 ml) room-temperature molasses

6 tablespoons plus 3 teaspoons extra-virgin olive or neutral oil, divided (3 tablespoons for dough, 3 teaspoons for oiling the bowl and coating the dough, and 3 tablespoons for oiling the baking sheet and coating the dough)

Finishing salt, to taste (optional)

Initial Mixing

1. In a large bowl, combine the flours, wheat bran, oats, cornmeal, cocoa powder, salt, and seeds and blend well. Set aside.

2. In a medium bowl, add the yeast to the room-temperature water and stir well to dissolve. Add the room-temperature molasses and 3 tablespoons of the oil and stir to blend. (If using a stand mixer, mix with the paddle attachment on low speed until combined.)

3. Make a well in the middle of the dry ingredients, then pour all the wet ingredients into the well. Using a Danish dough whisk or bowl scraper, blend by moving the dry ingredients into the middle to achieve a shaggy ball (page 19).

4. Cover and let rest in a warm, draft-free place for 15 minutes. This step is known as autolysis (page 16).

Multitask Moment

While the dough is resting, start gathering the other ingredients for your chosen project.

Dough Development and First Rise

1. Turn the dough out onto a lightly floured work surface and continue kneading for 8 to 10 minutes, until a smooth ball forms. The dough should feel firm yet slightly tacky to the touch.

2. Oil the bowl with 2 teaspoons of the oil.

3. Return the dough to the bowl, cover, and let rest in a warm, draft-free place for an additional 20 minutes.

Dough Development and Second Rise

1. Knead the dough again on a lightly floured surface for 10 minutes, forming a smooth ball that should now show slight elasticity.

2. Coat the dough with 1 teaspoon of the oil and cover the bowl. (If you need to start the recipe ahead of time, at this point the dough can be stored in an airtight container in the refrigerator for up to 48 hours.)

3. Allow the dough to proof, covered, in a warm, draft-free place for about 1 hour. The dough should be slightly smaller than double in size.

Multitask Moment

Begin to prepare the decorations for your chosen project.

Oven Preparation

This bread is baked at a lower temperature than the lean doughs due to the higher amounts of natural sugars. Thirty minutes prior to baking, move the oven rack to the middle and preheat the oven to 400°F (200°C; gas mark 6), allowing time for the oven to come to full temperature. I do not recommend using a baking stone for this bread.

Shaping

1. Line an 18 x 13-inch (46 x 33 cm) baking sheet with parchment paper and oil it well with 1 tablespoon of the oil.

2. Use a bowl scraper or oiled hand to gently transfer the dough to the middle of the sheet with the smooth side of the dough facing up. If the dough lands upside down, gently flip it over so that the smooth side is up.

3. With oiled fingers, begin spreading the dough out using a "cat" kneading motion— remember to keep your fingers open and bent like a piano player. Shape the dough into a rectangular dough "canvas," about 16 x 11 inches (41 x 28 cm), leaving space on all sides for expansion. If the dough is springing back, allow it to rest for 5 to 8 minutes. After this rest, the dough will be supple and ready for shaping again.

Decorating

1. Coat the dough with the remaining 2 tablespoons oil, then decorate the focaccia according to the directions of your chosen project.

2. Because this dough is slightly denser it will require a resting period after decorating. Place in a warm, draft-free place, lightly covered with a tea towel, for 15 minutes. Ultimately, you want to see an uneven bubbly texture, about 1½ to 2 inches (4 to 5 cm) thick in various spots. If the focaccia is flat, allow it to rest for 8 to 10 minutes in a warm, draft-free place.

Baking

1. Just before placing the focaccia in the oven, check the decorations to be sure they are all snug. Secure any that look to be popping off, using a chopstick, skewer, or your fingers.

2. Add finishing salt (if using) and place the focaccia on the middle rack.

3. Immediately reduce the oven temperature to 375°F (190°C; gas mark 5) and bake for 20 to 25 minutes, until the crust is deep brown.

4. Let cool until warm to the touch before cutting.

Sweet Focaccia

The smell of this bread baking will quickly populate your kitchen. This bread has a donut-like texture and is tender and slightly sweet, making this dough versatile for so many baking projects. To make rolling out and shaping easier, I recommend allowing the dough to rest in the refrigerator for the last 30 minutes of the final rise.

YIELD: 1 FOCACCIA

1 cup (240 ml) whole milk (or extra-creamy oat milk for a vegan alternative)

1 packet or 2¼ teaspoons (7 g) instant yeast

½ cup (112 ml) room-temperature water (70 to 72°F, or 21 to 22°C)

½ cup (100 g) granulated sugar

4½ cups (630 g) all-purpose flour

2 teaspoons (12 g) or 1 tablespoon plus 1 teaspoon (12 g) kosher salt

4 tablespoons unsalted butter (or vegan butter), softened, plus more for coating

1 tablespoon plus 1 teaspoon neutral oil (avoid using olive oil for this sweet dough), divided (1 teaspoon for coating the dough and 1 tablespoon for oiling the baking sheet)

Initial Mixing

1. Warm the milk on the stovetop in a pot to 72°F (22°C), just warm to the touch, not hot. Do not boil or scald.

2. Pour the warm milk into a medium bowl and add the yeast, water, and sugar. Whisk together until fully incorporated. (If using a stand mixer, mix with the paddle attachment.)

3. In a large bowl, blend the flour and salt and make a well in the middle.

4. Pour the milk mixture into the well and use a Danish dough whisk or bowl scraper to incorporate the flour into the liquid in the middle until a lumpy mass starts to form and all the flour has been absorbed. (If using a stand mixer, change to the dough hook attachment, add the dry ingredients to the wet ingredients, and mix on low speed until blended into a lumpy mass.)

5. Add 1 tablespoon of butter at a time and blend into the dough using one hand. Make sure it is fully blended before adding the next tablespoon of butter. Repeat until all butter has been incorporated. (If using a mixer, use the dough hook and add the butter, 1 tablespoon at a time, until all the butter is blended into the dough.)

6. Cover the bowl and let the dough rest in a warm, draft-free place for 15 minutes. This step is known as autolysis (page 16).

Multitask Moment

While the dough is resting, start gathering the other ingredients for your chosen project.

Dough Development and First Rise

1. Uncover the dough. Begin the first of two sets of stretch and folds (page 19), 10 to 12 times. Being an enriched dough, it is a bit softer and will not stretch as lean dough does. Just stretch enough to get the dough to fold over itself. (If using a stand mixer, use the dough hook and mix the dough on medium-low speed until the dough forms a smooth ball that comes off the sides of the bowl as a mass.)

2. Cover and let rest in a warm, draft-free place for an additional 15 minutes.

Dough Development and Second Rise

1. Uncover the rested dough and, with buttered fingers, repeat 10 to 12 stretch and folds. A smooth, somewhat elastic ball should now be formed. (If using a stand mixer, use the dough hook and mix the dough on medium speed for 6 to 7 minutes. The dough will now be very smooth and have a bit more elasticity.)

2. Lightly coat the bowl with butter.

3. Return the dough to the bowl and cover. Let the dough proof in a warm, draft-free place for 1½ hours. The dough should double in size. This dough can take longer to rise due to its ingredients. (If you need to start the recipe ahead of time, at this point the dough can be stored in an airtight container in the refrigerator for up to 48 hours. Lightly coat the dough in butter to ensure the dough does not dry out.)

4. For the last 30 minutes of the final proof, shape the dough into a tight ball, lightly coat the dough with 1 teaspoon of the oil, and place, covered, in the refrigerator to chill slightly. This makes rolling out and shaping easier, as the butter will firm up.

Multitask Moment

Begin to prepare the decorations for your chosen project.

Oven Preparation

Thirty minutes prior to baking, move the oven rack to the middle and preheat the oven to 350°F (180°C; gas mark 4), allowing time for the oven to come to full temperature. I do not recommend using a baking stone for this bread. The sugars and milk fats will cause the bread to burn quickly.

Shaping

1. Line an 18 x 13-inch (46 x 33 cm) baking sheet with parchment paper and oil it with the remaining 1 tablespoon oil.

2. Using a bowl scraper or oiled hand, gently transfer the dough to the middle of the sheet with the smooth side of the dough facing up. If the dough lands upside down, gently flip it over so that the smooth side is up.

3. Shape the dough into a rectangular dough "canvas," about 16 x 11 inches (41 x 28 cm), leaving space on all sides for expansion. Give the dough a very gentle dimple (page 17) to help create depth and texture. The key is not to over-dimple.

4. Let rest in a warm, draft-free place for 15 to 20 minutes.

Decorating

1. Decorate the focaccia according to the directions of your chosen project.

2. Once you have finished decorating, survey the surface and deflate any large air bubbles with a toothpick or skewer, leaving smaller ones intact. Give a few pokes all around the dough to level out the playing field, so to speak—this is called docking (page 17). Using piano-style finger motions, gently dimple the dough again.

3. Let rest, lightly covered with a tea towel, in a warm, draft-free place for 15 to 20 minutes. The dough should just about double to 2 inches (5 cm) thick.

Baking

1. Just before placing the focaccia in the oven, check the decorations to be sure they are all snug. Secure any that look to be popping off, using a chopstick, skewer, or your fingers.

2. Place the focaccia on the middle rack and bake for 25 to 28 minutes, until golden brown, checking the decorations after 8 minutes of baking time. If any decorations are popping off, carefully place them back on and return to oven for the rest of the baking time.

3. Let cool completely before cutting. Any leftovers should be stored in the refrigerator.

VARIATION: CHOCOLATE DOUGH

Blend in 3 tablespoons of dark cocoa powder and 2 tablespoons of granulated sugar with the flour and salt in step 3 of Initial Mixing.

Flowers

When we think of splendor in nature, nothing is more gorgeous than flowers. Their value goes far beyond their beauty. We present them to cheer people up, to express love, and to say I'm sorry. We capture their fragrance in perfumes, cleaners, and flavorings. Their splendor has been captured in famous artworks as well, and my first ever focaccia bread art was a simple flower design. I find that "flower walks" are beneficial for the body, soul, and mind, so pay special attention the next time you are out and about and do stop and smell the roses (as well as other flowers).

Poppy Field

My very first focaccia art project was of a poppy field. It was inspired by a drive to North Carolina, where I was dropping off my two youngest boys at college and beautiful flowers are planted along the medians of the highways. One evening when I was cutting up some mini sweet peppers for a salad, they reminded me of the poppies along the highway. I was inspired to arrange them with some other vegetables on some focaccia dough that was just about to go into the oven, and thus, my love for focaccia art was born.

YIELD: 1 FOCACCIA

1 recipe for Basic White Focaccia (page 30) or Basic Whole Wheat Focaccia (page 34)

3 tablespoons extra-virgin olive or neutral oil, divided

1 teaspoon lemon juice

Bowl of ice water

15 leaves basil

5 leaves parsley

10 to 14 chives (varying in length from 6 to 10 inches, or 15 to 25 cm) or 6 scallions

2 red mini sweet peppers

2 yellow mini sweet peppers

2 orange mini sweet peppers

8 pitted kalamata olives

2 tablespoons crumbled feta or goat cheese

Finishing salt, to taste (optional)

Dough Preparation
Prepare the dough according to the recipe instructions to its second rise.

Vegetable Preparation

1. Prepare two pieces of parchment about the size of your intended focaccia and lay them on two 18 x 13-inch (46 x 33 cm) baking sheets. Coat the parchment on one of the sheets with 1 tablespoon of the oil.

2. Add the lemon juice to the bowl of ice water to keep the greens bright. Place the basil and parsley in the ice water.

3. For the stems, if using chives, place them in the ice water. If using scallions, cut off ½ inch (1 cm) from the bottom of each one, then vertically slice down each scallion on the bias into 4 pieces. Place in the ice water.

4. Starting at the bottom ends of the peppers, slice off the bottom tips and reserve them for decorating. Cut the peppers into rings ¼ inch (6 mm) thick.

5. Pat the olives dry. Slice them in half, cutting some vertically and others horizontally.

6. Move all the vegetables to the unoiled baking sheet, keeping things separate and organized by color and sizes for ease of use during the decorating process. Remove the greens from the ice water and dry them well before placing on the baking sheet. Place the crumbled cheese on the baking sheet too.

Oven Preparation

Thirty minutes prior to baking, move the oven rack to the middle and preheat the oven to 450°F (230°C; gas mark 8), allowing time for the oven to come to full temperature.

Shaping and Decorating

1. On the oiled baking sheet, shape your dough while dimpling it (page 17) into a rectangular dough "canvas," about 16 x 11 inches (41 x 28 cm), then coat it with the remaining 2 tablespoons oil.

2. Starting with the chive or scallion stems, place some straight and others bent on top of the dough, to give depth and dimension. As you place each stem, "lock" it in place by pushing it down into the dough with a chopstick. To set them in place use the back end of the chopstick to push the stems down into the dough deeply, at the top and bottom and a few spots in between.

3. After the stems are in place, lay out the basil and parsley leaves in various positions along the stems. Now press in the pepper rings in various places, mixing the colors around the focaccia. Fill some of the peppers with crumbled cheese and others with the olive halves. You can also place some of the reserved pepper ends as centers.

4. Once you have finished decorating, survey the surface and deflate any large air bubbles with a toothpick or skewer, leaving smaller ones intact (docking). Using piano-style finger motions, gently dimple the dough again. Ultimately, you want to see an uneven bubbly texture, about 1½ to 2 inches (4 to 5 cm) thick in various spots. If the focaccia is flat, allow it to rest for 8 to 10 minutes in a warm, draft-free place.

Baking

1. Just before placing your focaccia in the oven, check the decorations to be sure they are all snug. Secure any that look to be popping off, using the chopstick, a skewer, or your fingers.

2. Add finishing salt (if using) and place the focaccia on the middle rack of the oven.

3. Bake for 8 minutes, then reduce the heat to 375°F (190°C; gas mark 5) and check the decorations again. If any are popping off, coerce them back into the dough by gently and carefully poking down. You don't want to burn yourself. Bake for 10 to 16 more minutes, until the focaccia is golden brown and crisp on the edges.

4. Remove from the oven and let cool for at least 5 to 10 minutes before cutting.

Sunflowers

This project was inspired by the majestic sunflower, the stalwart of the flower garden. They grow in early summer and last throughout the fall, not only emanating beauty but also providing food for the birds and bees. The most distinctive characteristic of the sunflower is its motion. They follow the sun, turning their faces toward its glow all day long.

YIELD: 1 FOCACCIA

1 recipe for Basic White Focaccia (page 30) or Basic Whole Wheat Focaccia (page 34)

3 tablespoons extra-virgin olive or neutral oil, divided

1 teaspoon lemon juice

Bowl of ice water

12 leaves basil

4 sprigs parsley

8 to 10 leaves arugula

4 scallions

8 yellow mini sweet peppers

4 orange mini sweet peppers

1 red mini sweet pepper

12 pitted black or kalamata olives

1 to 2 tablespoons mixed seeds (I used a combination of white and black sesame seeds or brown and golden flaxseeds)

Finishing salt, to taste (optional)

Dough Preparation

Prepare the dough according to the recipe instructions to its second rise.

Vegetable Preparation

1. Prepare two pieces of parchment about the size of your intended focaccia and lay them on two 18 x 13-inch (46 x 33 cm) baking sheets. Coat the parchment on one of the sheets with 1 tablespoon of the oil.

2. Add the lemon juice to the bowl of ice water to keep the greens bright. Place the basil, parsley, and arugula in the ice water.

3. For the stems, cut off ½ inch (1 cm) from the bottom of each scallion, and then vertically slice down each scallion on the bias into 4 pieces. Place in the ice water.

4. Cut off the tops of the peppers about 1 inch (2.5 cm) down from the top.
   Cut out the stems from the pepper tops, then turn the tops onto their sides on the cutting board and use small cuts to fray the edges. Place the frayed tops in the ice water to help the fraying expand. They will expand more the longer they stay in the water.

5. Cut the bottom tips off the peppers and set aside. Slice the peppers in half lengthwise, then slice some of the pepper halves lengthwise into long thin strips and others crosswise for shorter strips. The ones cut crosswise should have a nice curve to them.

6. Pat the olives dry. Chop most of them into small pieces, but reserve 2 or 3 whole ones.

7. Move all the vegetables to the unoiled baking sheet, keeping things separate and organized by color and sizes for ease of use during the decorating process. Remove the greens and the pepper tops from the ice water and dry them well before placing on the sheet. Place the seeds on the baking sheet too.

Oven Preparation

Thirty minutes prior to baking, move the oven rack to the middle and preheat the oven to 450°F (230°C; gas mark 8), allowing time for the oven to come to full temperature.

Shaping and Decorating

1. On the oiled baking sheet, shape your dough while dimpling it (page 17) into a rectangular dough "canvas," about 16 x 11 inches (41 x 28 cm), then coat it with the remaining 2 tablespoons oil.

2. Starting with the scallion stems, find the firmest pieces and create a nice arrangement on your focaccia, overcrowding as you go, as you can always pull some off. Some scallions will have a natural curl; these look great around the base of the stem arrangement and intertwined through the longer, straighter stems. As you place each stem, "lock" it in place by pushing it down into the dough with a chopstick. To set them in place use the back end of the chopstick to push the stems down into the dough deeply, at the top and bottom and a few spots in between.

3. Place a teaspoon of the chopped olives at the top of the first stem, then begin placing pepper strips as petals around the olives. Make sure they are touching each other as the dough will expand. You can mix up the colors as well to give a little contrast to the flowers. Continue doing this around your dough canvas until the picture is full, placing large and small flowers all over the surface.

4. You can also use the frayed pepper tops for smaller flowers, placing them on a shorter stem with a whole olive in the middle. Just be sure to dry the soaked peppers well before placing them on the dough. The reserved pepper tips are great to use for unopened buds on shorter stems.

5. Place the basil, parsley, and arugula leaves in spaces where they look most appealing in your design. Use parsley leaves around the base of each flower and secure all the leaves by poking them into the dough using the end of a chopstick. Avoid getting too much oil on the leaves. After the leaves are tucked into the dough, wet your fingers with water and dampen the tops of the leaves; this will help them stay green while baking.

6. Scatter some mixed seeds across the bottom section of the dough to finish.

7. Once you have finished decorating, survey the surface and deflate any large air bubbles with a toothpick or skewer, leaving smaller ones intact (docking). Using piano-style finger motions, gently dimple the dough again. Ultimately, you want to see an uneven bubbly texture, about 1½ to 2 inches (4 to 5 cm) thick in various spots. If the focaccia is flat, allow it to rest for 8 to 10 minutes in a warm, draft-free place.

Baking

1. Just before placing your focaccia in the oven, check the decorations to be sure they are all snug. Secure any that look to be popping off, using the chopstick, a skewer, or your fingers. Dimple the dough again, if needed.

2. Add finishing salt (if using) and place the focaccia on the middle rack of the oven.

3. Bake for 8 minutes at 450°F (230°C; gas mark 8). Reduce the heat to 375°F (190°C; gas mark 5) and check the decorations again. If any are popping off, coerce them back into the dough by gently and carefully poking down. You don't want to burn yourself. Bake for 10 to 16 more minutes, until the focaccia is golden brown and crisp on the edges.

4. Remove from the oven and let cool for at least 5 to 10 minutes before cutting.

VARIATION: SUNFLOWERS WITH WOVEN VASE

Reserve a golf ball–size piece of dough before shaping the focaccia and set it aside. Follow the directions as above for creating the sunflower design, except the stems should be positioned toward the middle with a space left underneath. If you desire to add color to your vase, lay a piece of roasted red pepper that has been dried with a paper towel and cut into a 3-inch (7.5 cm) circle over the bottom part of the stems, slightly tucking the edges of the pepper into the dough. Roll out the reserved dough to about ¼ inch (6 mm) thick. Brush the dough with water and dust with dark cocoa powder to cover. Lattice-cut the dough if you have a lattice cutter; otherwise cut the dough into ¼-inch-wide (6 mm) strips and place them on an angle and weave the strips together (follow the directions on page 26 for latticework). Lay the lattice over the top of the red pepper (if using), stretching it slightly to reveal the red color underneath and tucking the sides into the dough of your focaccia slightly. Shape the lattice with a narrow top surrounding the flower stems by pinching in the dough around the stems about 3 inches (7.5 cm) up from the base so that you have a vase shape. Tidy up the lattice into a bowl shape by slightly tucking the ends into the dough. Round the shape by cupping your hands and laying them around the circumference of the lattice dough.

Wrapped Bouquet

This is such a pretty presentation. Taking inspiration from a colorful bouquet, this focaccia has everything a lovely bouquet of flowers has but also the bonus of being deliciously edible. The ingredients listed below are for a variety of flowers, but feel free to choose your favorite flower types and style.

YIELD: 1 FOCACCIA

1 recipe for Basic White Focaccia (page 30) or Basic Whole Wheat Focaccia (page 34)

1 tablespoon cocoa powder, for coloring dough (optional)

2 tablespoons extra-virgin olive or neutral oil, divided

1 teaspoon lemon juice

Bowl of ice water

3 sprigs parsley

6 leaves basil

10 leaves arugula

1 whole roasted red pepper (see page 25 for how to roast your own)

6 pitted black olives

3 pitted kalamata olives

2 red mini sweet peppers

2 yellow mini sweet peppers

2 orange mini sweet peppers

1 medium oval-shaped red onion

1 small leek

2 small purple potatoes

3 scallions

20 capers, rinsed

36 pine nuts or sunflower seeds

2 tablespoons crumbled feta or goat cheese

Finishing salt, to taste (optional)

Special Tools

Mini flower-shaped cookie cutters

Lattice cutter (optional)

Dough Preparation

1. Prepare the dough according to the recipe instructions to before its second rise.

2. Trim off 2 small portions of dough, both slightly larger than a golf ball for the latticework (see Note on page 58). Knead the cocoa powder into one of the portions to create a dark brown dough for contrast. Form both portions into small balls, cover, and let rest in a warm, draft-free place, along with the larger dough ball.

3. Form the remaining dough into a smooth ball, cover, and let proof (second rise) for 1 hour in a warm, draft-free place .

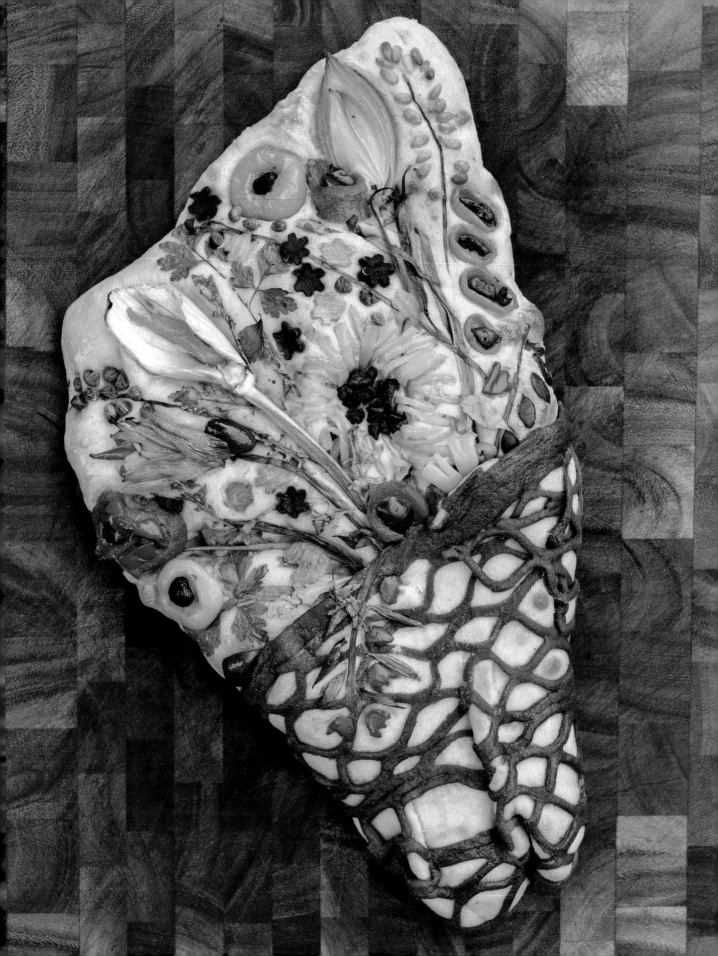

Vegetable Preparation

1. Prepare two pieces of parchment about the size of your intended focaccia and lay them on two 18 x 13-inch (46 x 33 cm) baking sheets. Coat the parchment on one of the sheets with 1 tablespoon of the oil.

2. Add the lemon juice to the bowl of ice water to keep the greens bright. Place the basil, parsley, and arugula in the ice water.

3. Cut the roasted red pepper into 3 long thin strips, about ¾ inch (2 cm) wide. Pat the olives dry. Chop the black ones into small pieces and slice the kalamata olives in half lengthwise.

4. Cut off the bottom tips from the mini peppers and reserve them for the flower centers. Cut about 1 inch (2.5 cm) down from the top of each mini pepper and remove the seeds and pith. Cut out the stems from the pepper tops, then turn the tops onto their sides on the cutting board and use small cuts to fray the edges. Place the frayed tops in the ice water to help the fraying expand. Cut the middles of the yellow mini peppers into matchsticks to be used for the sunflower petals and 1 orange mini pepper into rings. Slice the red mini peppers in half lengthwise. Flatten the pepper halves and use the small flower cutters to cut out shapes from some of the flattened pieces.

5. Place the onion on a cutting board with the bottom part down. Using a sharp knife, slice the onion in half from top to root, then slice a ¼-inch-thick (6 mm) slice from one of the cut sides lengthwise. Trim away the outer layers until you have a closed bud-like flower from the center part of the onion, approximately 1 to 2 inches (2.5 to 5 cm) wide.

6. Follow the directions for making a calla lily from a leek layer (see Making the Cut on page 23). The green parts of the leek can be used to make lovely oblong leaves. Soak them in the ice water until ready to use. From the remaining orange pepper, cut a narrow triangle that is 2 inches (5 cm) long for the stamen (center) of the calla lily.

7. Use the mini flower cutters to cut out shapes from the purple potatoes and red onions (see Making the Cut on page 24).

8. For the stems, cut off ½ inch (1 cm) from the bottom of each scallion, and then vertically slice down each scallion on the bias into strips ½ inch (1 cm) wide. Place in the ice water.

9. Move all the vegetables to the unoiled baking sheet, keeping things separate and organized by color and sizes for ease of use during the decorating process. Remove the greens from the ice water and dry them well before placing on the baking sheet. Place the crumbled cheese, olives, capers, and pine nuts on the baking sheet too.

Oven Preparation

Thirty minutes prior to baking, move the oven rack to the middle and preheat the oven to 450°F (230°C; gas mark 8), allowing time for the oven to come to full temperature.

Shaping

1. Shape the dough while dimpling it (page 17) into a rough triangle shape, about 13 inches (33 cm) long on the left side, 15 inches (38 cm) long on the right side, and 10 inches (25 cm) at its widest point. Give a tug to one side and pull down from the bottom. Work lengthwise on your oiled baking sheet so that you have a tall bouquet shape. The dough will easily take shape as you nudge it along.

2. Coat the dough with the remaining 2 tablespoons oil.

Decorating

1. Position the scallion stems on the dough, gathering them at the bottom right of the heart and spreading them out across the top in various directions to fill the space. Add the leek leaves around the stems. As you place each stem, "lock" it in place by pushing it down into the dough with a chopstick. To set them in place use the back end of the chopstick to push the stems down into the dough deeply, at the top and bottom and a few spots in between.

2. Use the seeds and capers to add buds to the long thin stems.

3. Make a small notch in your dough to hold each rose. Using kitchen scissors, snip a ½-inch (1 cm) X shape in the spots where you will be positioning the roses. Do not cut through the dough, but cut just deep enough to make a small opening to snugly place the roses.

4. Pat the red pepper strips dry. Wrap one around your finger, with the inside portion of the pepper facing outward. Carefully move it off your finger and place the curled-up pepper in position as a rose. Secure it by gently pressing it into the small notch you just made. Continue wrapping and placing the roses with the remaining red pepper strips. Bend the edges of each rose so that they curl over slightly to resemble petals.

5. Make a sunflower with the yellow pepper matchsticks in the center of the bouquet with the chopped black olives for its center. Use the tips and rings of the mini peppers as other flower shapes, with kalamata olive halves in the centers. Place the different flowers randomly around the dough, crowding them together and overlapping to create a full bouquet. Fill in the design with the small flower cutouts from the mini peppers, potatoes, and onions and make different flower shapes with the onion layers and long leek layers.

6. Finally make the lattice. Roll out the brown dough and the plain dough on a lightly floured surface into two 6-inch (15 cm) squares. Use a lattice cutter if

you have one on the brown dough to make the lattice surface. If not, follow the directions on page 26 for latticework. Wet the lattice with a little water as needed to adhere the dark brown dough piece to the plain dough piece. The edges do not have to line up perfectly; the lattice may stretch out and lose its perfect form, which is perfectly fine. This is meant to represent decorative wrapping paper around the bouquet.

7. Once you have created the layered lattice "wrapping paper," transfer it to the focaccia and lay it over the bottom half of the focaccia, covering the stems at an angle, and making folds to represent paper wrapping. Tuck the ends underneath the focaccia dough.

8. You can place some "loose" flowers across the lattice for depth and interest.

9. Once you have finished decorating, survey the surface and deflate any large air bubbles with a toothpick or skewer, leaving smaller ones intact (docking). Using piano-style finger motions, gently dimple the dough again. Ultimately, you want to see an uneven bubbly texture, about 1½ to 2 inches (4 to 5 cm) thick in various spots. If the focaccia is flat, allow it to rest for 8 to 10 minutes in a warm, draft-free place.

Baking

1. Just before placing your focaccia in the oven, check the decorations to be sure they are all snug. Secure any that look to be popping off, using the chopstick, a skewer, or your fingers.

2. Add finishing salt (if using) and place the focaccia on the middle rack of the oven.

3. Bake for 8 minutes at 450°F (230°C; gas mark 8). Reduce the heat to 375°F (190°C; gas mark 5) and check the decorations again. If any are popping off, coerce them back into the dough by gently and carefully poking down. You don't want to burn yourself. Bake for 10 to 16 more minutes, until the focaccia is golden brown and crisp on the edges.

4. Remove from the oven and let cool for at least 5 to 10 minutes before cutting.

NOTE

If you would prefer not to use the lattice decoration, you don't need to set aside dough for it. You can simply stretch the bottom of the dough on both the left and right sides and fold them over the stems at the bottom, so the flowers look wrapped. Pinch the dough together to adhere the two sides together. If the dough is dry and not sticking together, wet the ends slightly, then pinch together.

Spring Tulips

One of the first signs of spring, tulips in all their colorful incarnations are the inspiration for this focaccia. They are always a welcome sight after a gray and snowy New England winter.

YIELD: 1 FOCACCIA

1 recipe for Basic White Focaccia (page 30) or Basic Whole Wheat Focaccia (page 34)

3 tablespoons extra-virgin olive or neutral oil, divided

1 teaspoon lemon juice

Bowl of ice water

1 small or medium leek

2 red mini sweet peppers

2 yellow mini sweet peppers

2 orange mini sweet peppers

1 small or medium red onion

Finishing salt, to taste (optional)

Dough Preparation

Prepare the dough according to the recipe instructions to its second rise.

Vegetable Preparation

1. Prepare two pieces of parchment about the size of your intended focaccia and lay them on two 18 x 13-inch (46 x 33 cm) baking sheets. Coat the parchment on one of the sheets with 1 tablespoon of the oil.

2. Add the lemon juice to the bowl of ice water to keep the greens bright.

3. For the stems, make a slit lengthwise down the leek and remove and discard the outer layer. Separate out the layers and wash each one under cold water to remove any dirt and sand. Dry and place on a cutting board. Using a paring knife, cut down the length of each layer on the greener parts creating 13 or 14 stems that are ½ inch (1 cm) wide and in varying lengths from 4 to 8 inches (10 to 20 cm). Cut long leaf shapes using the paring knife. Run the knife in a curving motion down the green part and taper at the end. Make 10 to 12 leaves of varying length of 4 to 8 inches (10 to 20 cm). Place the stems and leaves in the ice water.

4. Cut each pepper in half lengthwise and remove the seeds and pith. Lay the first pepper half on a cutting board with the interior side facing up. With a paring knife, carve petals into the top edge of the pepper by making 1-inch-deep (2.5 cm) and narrow V-shaped slits, spaced about ¼ inch (6 mm) apart. Each pepper half should have anywhere from 3 to 5 petals depending on the size. Repeat with all colors of peppers until you have 8 to 10 good tulips.

5. Remove and discard the outer layer from the red onion. Separate out some more layers and use a paring knife to cut 5 tulip shapes, curved at the bottom and zigzagged at the top.

6. Move all the vegetables to the unoiled baking sheet, keeping things separate and organized by color and sizes for ease of use during the decorating process. Remove the green stems from the ice water and dry them well before placing on the baking sheet.

Oven Preparation

Thirty minutes prior to baking, move the oven rack to the middle and preheat the oven to 450°F (230°C; gas mark 8), allowing time for the oven to come to full temperature.

Shaping and Decorating

1. On the oiled baking sheet, shape your dough while dimpling it (page 17) into a rectangular dough "canvas," about 16 x 11 inches (41 x 28 cm), then coat it with the remaining 2 tablespoons oil.

2. Place the stems at different lengths and in different directions on the focaccia dough. Place the leaves, overlapping the stems at the top and bottom. As you place each stem, "lock" it in place by pushing it down into the dough with a chopstick. To set them in place use the back end of the chopstick to push the stems down into the dough deeply, at the top and bottom and a few spots in between.

3. Arrange the pepper and onion tulips at the tops of the stems across the dough, mixing up the colors.

4. Once you have finished decorating, survey the surface and deflate any large air bubbles with a toothpick or skewer, leaving smaller ones intact (docking). Using piano-style finger motions, gently dimple the dough again. Ultimately, you want to see an uneven bubbly texture, about 1½ to 2 inches (4 to 5 cm) thick in various spots. If the focaccia is flat, allow it to rest for 8 to 10 minutes in a warm, draft-free place.

Baking

1. Just before placing your focaccia in the oven, check the decorations to be sure they are all snug. Secure any that look to be popping off, using the chopstick, a skewer, or your fingers.

2. Add finishing salt (if using) and place the focaccia on the middle rack of the oven.

3. Bake for 8 minutes at 450°F (230°C; gas mark 8). Reduce the heat to 375°F (190°C; gas mark 5) and check the decorations again. If any are popping off, coerce them back into the dough by gently and carefully poking down. You don't want to burn yourself. Bake for 10 to 16 more minutes, until the focaccia is golden brown and crisp on the edges.

4. Remove from the oven and let cool for at least 5 to 10 minutes before cutting.

White Irises in a Vase

Elevate the flavor of this focaccia even more by adding a flavor variation to the basic dough recipe. This simple design could be done with any color of onion you like. I made this focaccia with a red, or purple, onion, and it was quite stunning and tasty. The key is to choose an onion that has a wide oval shape.

YIELD: 1 FOCACCIA

1 recipe for Basic White Focaccia (page 30) with a flavor variation of kalamata olive, rosemary, and poppy seed (page 33)

3 tablespoons extra-virgin olive or neutral oil, divided

1 large white onion (choose one that has a wide oval shape)

4 large scallions

½ cup (120 g) Basil Pesto (page 169) or Evergreen Sauce (page 168)

Finishing salt, to taste (optional)

Dough Preparation

Prepare the dough according to the recipe instructions to its second rise.

Vegetable Preparation

1. Prepare two pieces of parchment about the size of your intended focaccia and lay them on two 18 x 13-inch (46 x 33 cm) baking sheets. Coat the parchment on one of the sheets with 1 tablespoon of the oil.

2. Remove any dry papery skin from the outside of the onion. The root of the onion plays a roll in holding the onion together, so while you work, do not carve it away. Place the onion on a cutting board with the root end down.

3. To make the bulb vase, slice the onion in half vertically from the top center (neck end) to the root. Wrap up one-half of the onion and store in the refrigerator for another use. Stand up the remaining half vertically as before, with the root on the cutting board. Make a ½-inch (1 cm) slice vertically, keeping the layers intact at the root. Set the larger portion aside, and lay the slice on the cutting board, revealing white blossom-like layers attached at the bottom by the root area. Cut off any dry tips at the neck. Make a small half-moon notch in the root area of the slice, but do not completely remove the root area. This will help to hold the layers together. Carefully set aside. You may need to use a spatula to move it, depending on how much root is left on the bottom, which will actually be the top when you place it on the dough.

4. To make the flower petals, lay the remaining onion half, root still intact, flat side down, on the cutting board. Using a small paring knife, cut the onion in half, root to neck, and then cut those halves in half for 4 wedges of layered onion. Separate each wedge into sections of 2 or 3 layers, leaving the root intact, if possible, so that they stay together. With the small paring knife, make a zigzag cut lengthwise on the outer edges of each cluster of layers to create 12 to 14 iris-like petals of varying sizes.

5. To make the flower centers, with the remaining pieces of onion, cut three 2-inch-wide (5 cm) ovals. Make the tops and sides jagged by notching the pieces with the paring knife to create a crepe-like effect. Leave the bottom part smooth.

6. Cut off the bottom of each scallion about ½ inch (6 cm) from the base, then cut the scallions in half lengthwise. Place 3 trimmed scallions aside for stems. Use the last one to create 2 pointed leaves, about 4 inches (10 cm) long, using scissors or a paring knife.

7. Move all the vegetables to the unoiled baking sheet, keeping things separate and organized by color and sizes for ease of use during the decorating process.

Oven Preparation

Thirty minutes prior to baking, move the oven rack to the middle and preheat the oven to 450°F (230°C; gas mark 8), allowing time for the oven to come to full temperature.

Shaping and Decorating

1. On the oiled baking sheet, shape your dough while dimpling it (page 17) into a rectangular dough "canvas," about 16 x 11 inches (41 x 28 cm), then coat it with the remaining 2 tablespoons oil, leaving the area where the Basil Pesto will be spread uncoated.

2. Place the stems off-center on the right side of your focaccia dough, with the pointed leaves at the left of the stems, leaving about 4 inches (10 cm) of space at the top. Gather the stems and leaves together at the bottom. If necessary, trim to fit. As you place each stem and leaf, "lock" it in place by pushing it down into the dough with a chopstick. To set them in place use the back end of the chopstick to push the stems down into the dough deeply, at the top and bottom and a few spots in between.

3. Place the onion bulb vase on the dough over the stems with the root side at the top and the neck as the base. Try to center the stems into the small oval notch you made in the root, then tuck the vase into the dough so that it is snug.

4. Use a small spoon to spread the pesto or evergreen sauce over the bottom third of the focaccia dough. Lay down a chopstick where you want the green area to stop on the dough to keep a straight line. Spread carefully around the onion bulb.

5. Place 4 curved petals on each stem around the flower centers, with 2 petals on the right and 2 on the left drooping down. Press the petals into the dough to secure them. For more depth, you can position a couple of the petals over the stems.

6. Once you have finished decorating, survey the surface and deflate any large air bubbles with a toothpick or skewer, leaving smaller ones intact (docking). Using piano-style finger motions, gently dimple the dough again. Ultimately, you want to see an uneven bubbly texture, about 1½ to 2 inches (4 to 5 cm) thick in various spots. If the focaccia is flat, allow it to rest for 8 to 10 minutes in a warm, draft-free place.

Baking

1. Just before placing your focaccia in the oven, check the decorations to be sure they are all snug. Secure any that look to be popping off, using the chopstick, a skewer, or your fingers.

2. Add finishing salt (if using) and place the focaccia on the middle rack of the oven.

3. Bake for 8 minutes at 450°F (230°C; gas mark 8). Reduce the heat to 375°F (190°C; gas mark 5) and check the decorations again. If any are popping off, coerce them back into the dough by gently and carefully poking down. You don't want to burn yourself. Bake for 10 to 16 more minutes, until the focaccia is golden brown and crisp on the edges.

4. Remove from the oven and let cool for at least 5 to 10 minutes before cutting.

Dahlias

This ombré focaccia makes such a pretty presentation, and the addition of warm, melting Brie in the center is a festive way to serve cheese.

YIELD: 1 FOCACCIA

1 recipe for Basic White Focaccia (page 30) or Basic Whole Wheat Focaccia (page 34)

3 tablespoons plus 3 teaspoons extra-virgin olive or neutral oil, divided

1 teaspoon lemon juice

Bowl of ice water

4 to 6 sprigs parsley

1 large red bell pepper (choose one with deep crevices)

1 large yellow bell pepper (choose one with deep crevices)

1 large orange bell pepper (choose one with deep crevices)

1 recipe for Sun-Dried Tomato Pesto (page 169)

1 small container multicolored grape tomatoes (with at least 14 orange ones)

1 round (8 ounces, or 227 g) Brie cheese

Olive oil, for coating the Brie

Fresh chopped thyme or rosemary, to taste (optional)

2 tablespoons chutney of your choice (optional)

Finishing salt, to taste (optional)

Special Tools

1 (8-ounce, or 240-ml) ramekin (4 inches, or 20 cm, in size)

Dough Preparation

Prepare the dough according to the recipe instructions to its second rise.

Vegetable Preparation

1. Prepare two pieces of parchment about the size of your intended focaccia and lay them on two 18 x 13-inch (46 x 33 cm) baking sheets. Coat the parchment on one of the sheets with 1 tablespoon of the oil.

2. Add the lemon juice to the bowl of ice water to keep the greens bright. Place the parsley in the ice water.

3. Cut the peppers in half lengthwise, then cut each pepper half crosswise into ½ inch (1 cm) slices so that they form a C shape.

4. Move all the vegetables to the unoiled baking sheet, keeping things separate and organized by color and sizes for ease of use during the decorating process. Remove the greens from the ice water and dry them well before placing on the baking sheet.

Oven Preparation

Thirty minutes prior to baking, move the oven rack to the middle and preheat the oven to 450°F (230°C; gas mark 8), allowing time for the oven to come to full temperature.

Shaping

1. The easiest way to create a perfectly round focaccia is to shape the dough during the last 30 minutes of the second rise into a smooth ball. Gently turn the dough out onto a slightly damp work surface and begin by pulling the dough on opposite sides over each other, pinching together, and then repeating on the other sides. Flip over the dough to the smooth side. Tuck slightly damp, cupped hands behind the dough and pull it toward your torso while pressing your hands along the work surface for about 6 to 8 inches (15 to 20 cm) in length, tucking in and tightening the dough as you drag. Repeat this same motion and hand position, only this time to the right of the dough. Repeat on all sides, tightening the dough into a smooth ball as you drag your cupped hands across it. Dampen your hands as necessary, and it may be useful to moisten the work surface if the dough does not have enough friction when moved across the surface. Once you have achieved a fairly tight round ball, carefully transfer the ball, smooth side up, to the oiled baking sheet.

2. Rub 1 teaspoon of the oil over the top surface of the dough and cover with an inverted bowl to rise under. If the bowl is too big for the baking sheet, cover the dough with a damp cloth. Let rest for 20 minutes in a warm, draft-free place. After 20 minutes, begin dimpling the dough with oiled fingers and shape into a round focaccia that is about 12 inches (30 cm) in diameter and 1½ to 2 inches (4 to 5 cm) thick. Coat the dough with 2 tablespoons of the oil.

3. Coat both sides of a square of parchment paper to fit underneath the ramekin with 1 teaspoon of the oil. Place the parchment and ramekin in the center of the dough and firmly press down the ramekin into the dough, but not too hard that it cuts through it. This will be a placeholder and create a well for the cheese.

Decorating

1. Starting from the ramekin, place 7 or 8 red C-shaped peppers, facing inward toward the ramekin and touching each other, and form a ring around the ramekin. Place about 11 or 12 orange C-shaped peppers, as you did the red peppers, in a ring around the red peppers. Place about 14 yellow C-shaped peppers in a ring around the orange peppers, completing the flower.

2. Use a small spoon to fill the insides of the red and orange peppers with sun-dried tomato pesto. Place the small orange grape tomatoes inside the yellow peppers.

3. Place about 12 to 15 sets of parsley leaves, preferably 3 leaves to each stem, around the outside of the flower petals to fill space.

4. Leave the ramekin in place for the entire bake.

5. Once you have finished decorating, survey the surface and deflate any large air bubbles with a toothpick or skewer, leaving smaller ones intact (docking). Using piano-style finger motions, gently dimple the dough again. Ultimately, you want to see an uneven bubbly texture, about 1½ to 2 inches (4 to 5 cm) thick in various spots. If the focaccia is flat, allow it to rest for 8 to 10 minutes in a warm, draft-free place.

6. Meanwhile, using the container the Brie came in as a stencil, mark and cut a piece of round parchment paper that is slightly bigger than the Brie. Lightly coat one side of the parchment with the remaining 1 teaspoon oil and place under the Brie round on a baking sheet. This will be used to transfer the baked cheese to the focaccia later. Lightly coat the cheese with olive oil and season with fresh herbs (if using). Spoon the chutney on top (if using). Set aside.

Baking

1. Just before placing your focaccia in the oven, check the decorations to be sure they are all snug. Secure any that look to be popping off, using a chopstick, skewer, or your fingers.

2. Add finishing salt (if using) and place the focaccia on the middle rack of the oven.

3. Bake for 8 minutes at 450°F (230°C; gas mark 8). Reduce the heat to 375°F (190°C; gas mark 5) and check the decorations again. If any are popping off, coerce them back into the dough by gently and carefully poking down. You don't want to burn yourself. Bake for 10 to 16 more minutes, until the focaccia is golden brown and crisp on the edges. Remove from oven and allow to cool for 8 to 10 minutes.

4. Meanwhile, place the Brie in the oven at 375°F (190°C; gas mark 5) for 8 to 10 minutes while the focaccia is cooling. The Brie will turn crisp and brown on the outside and just start to crack when ready. Immediately remove from the oven.

5. Place the focaccia on a serving board and carefully remove the ramekin and parchment underneath it. Using a spatula, slide the hot Brie into the center where the ramekin left a well, being careful not to disrupt the toasted skin of the cheese. Serve immediately.

6. Serve with a small bread knife or slice the bread as desired and dip it into the melty goodness. (Note: If you are not serving the bread until later, do not bake the cheese until you are ready to serve. Reheat the bread for 5 minutes just before serving.)

Cherry Blossoms

Cherry blossoms are synonymous with spring. The enchanting pink and white feathery flowers are a sign of warmer days ahead. This sweet focaccia is inspired by a trip to the National Cherry Blossom Festival held in Washington, DC, every spring and is perfect for serving at brunch or an afternoon tea.

YIELD: 1 FOCACCIA

1 recipe for Sweet Focaccia (page 41)

1 tablespoon neutral oil

12 strawberries

11 blueberries or pitted cherries, halved

14 pitted dried dates

2 sprigs mint leaves or 6 green grapes

Flour, for dusting

1 recipe for Sweet Lemon Cream (page 167)

10 to 12 sliced almonds

Egg wash (1 egg mixed with ¼ cup, or 60 ml, water) or whole milk, for brushing (optional)

Sparkling sugar, for sprinkling (optional)

Cinnamon "Wooden" Frame (optional)

1 cup (208 g) Cinnamon Filling (page 167)

Dough Preparation

Prepare the dough according to the recipe instructions to when it is chilling in the refrigerator for the last 30 minutes of the second rise.

Fruit Preparation

1. Prepare two pieces of parchment about the size of your intended focaccia and lay them on two 18 x 13-inch (46 x 33 cm) baking sheets. Coat the parchment on one of the sheets with the oil.

2. Remove and discard the strawberry tops. Position a strawberry with the top end on the cutting board. Using a paring knife, make narrow V-shaped notches lengthwise down the side of the strawberry. Depending on the size, you can get 4 or 5 notches. Be careful not to hit the center of the strawberry or the flower will fall apart as you slice it. The notches should only be about ¾ inch (2 cm) deep at the most. Turn the strawberry onto its side and cut it crosswise into ¼-inch-thick (6 mm) slices. These will be the flowers and will vary in size. Repeat with the remaining strawberries.

3. Slice the blueberries in half crosswise. These will be the centers of the flowers.

4. Slice the dates in half lengthwise, then cut each half lengthwise into 4 slices. These will be the stems and branches.

5. If using mint, discard the stems and use the smallest leaves. If using grapes, slice them in half lengthwise and then each half lengthwise again. Lay them on a paper towel to absorb any extra juices.

6. Move all the prepared fruit to the unoiled baking sheet, keeping things separate and organized by color and sizes for ease of use during the decorating process.

Oven Preparation

Thirty minutes prior to baking, move the oven rack to the middle and preheat the oven to 350°F (180°C; gas mark 4), allowing time for the oven to come to full temperature.

Shaping and Decorating

1. Place the chilled dough on a lightly floured surface. If adding the cinnamon "wooden" frame, cut off one-third of the dough and set aside. Use a rolling pin to roll out the larger piece of dough to a 10 x 7-inch (25 x 18 cm) rectangle. If not adding the cinnamon "wooden" frame, roll out the dough to a 14 x 8-inch (36 x 20 cm) rectangle. This dough should be fairly easy to roll out due to the enriched ingredients and not spring back too much.

2. Place the shaped dough on the oiled baking sheet and brush off any excess flour.

3. Spread a coat of the sweet lemon cream over the surface, about ¼ inch (6 mm) thick, leaving an uncoated ¾-inch (2 cm) space around all the edges. If you are adding the "wooden" frame, you need to add it now before continuing with the decorating (see opposite for instructions).

4. Create a tree with branches with the sliced dates, spreading them from the bottom right corner and up and across the dough.

5. Lay the mint leaves or grapes on the branches in various spots.

6. Gently place all the strawberry flowers around the branches so that they are full of blossoms. As you place them, some of the strawberry petals may come apart, so simply coerce them into place using tweezers or a toothpick.

7. Place the almond slices around the branches and strawberry flowers.

8. Once you have finished decorating, survey the surface and deflate any large air bubbles with a toothpick or skewer, leaving smaller ones intact (docking). Using piano-style finger motions, gently dimple the dough again. Do not over-dimple

9. Let rest, lightly covered with a tea towel, in a warm, draft-free place for 15 to 20 minutes. The dough should just about double to 2 inches (5 cm) thick.

Making the Cinnamon "Wooden" Frame (optional)

1. Roll out the reserved third of dough on a lightly floured surface. Roll the dough into a 22 x 6-inch (56 x 15 cm) rectangle.

2. Spritz the surface very lightly with water, then sprinkle liberally with the cinnamon filling, leaving ½ inch (1 cm) uncovered at the top to seal.

3. With the dough positioned lengthwise on your work space, roll it upward into a tight log, starting from the bottom-left side, to create a cinnamon swirl. Keep the dough even as you roll it into a log. Pinch the seam closed and roll the log slightly back and forth with your palms to ensure that it is even. With a knife, cut the entire log in half lengthwise, exposing the contrasting layers of dough and cinnamon. Slice each half down the center lengthwise for a total of 4 pieces.

4. Wet the edges of your focaccia, then place one of the cinnamon pieces alongside and up against one of the sides of the focaccia, making sure that the cut side is face up so that the layers of cinnamon and dough are exposed. Leave 2 inches (5 cm) of dough extended beyond the length of the focaccia side on each end of the piece for twisting later. You can stretch the cinnamon piece if needed for it to fit. Repeat with the remaining pieces. Twist each corner together by crossing the ends over one other and curling each end inward toward the frame.

Baking

1. If desired, create a shine by brushing the dough areas with egg wash or whole milk just prior to baking. Sprinkle with some sparkling sugar to finish.

2. Just before placing your focaccia in the oven, check the decorations to be sure they are all snug. Secure any that look to be popping off, using a chopstick, skewer, or your fingers.

3. Place the focaccia on the middle rack and bake for 25 to 28 minutes, until golden brown, checking the decorations after 8 minutes of baking time. If any decorations are popping off, carefully place them back on and return to oven for the rest of the baking time.

4. Remove from the oven and let cool until warm to the touch before cutting. Any leftovers should be stored in the refrigerator.

Bouquet of Calla Lilies

Though simplistic in their shape, these lilies bring elegance to any special occasion. The leeks shimmer and shine on top of the warm golden bread, adding flavor as well as beauty.

YIELD: 1 FOCACCIA

1 recipe for Basic White Focaccia (page 30) or Basic Whole Wheat Focaccia (page 34)

3 tablespoons extra-virgin olive or neutral oil, divided

2 large leeks with longer green parts

6 whole baby corns (canned is fine) or 2 orange mini sweet peppers

1 teaspoon lemon juice

Bowl of ice water

1 large whole roasted red pepper (see page 25 for how to roast your own)

Finishing salt, to taste (optional)

Dough Preparation

Prepare the dough according to the recipe instructions to its second rise.

Vegetable Preparation

1. Prepare two pieces of parchment about the size of your intended focaccia and lay them on two 18 x 13-inch (46 x 33 cm) baking sheets. Coat the parchment on one of the sheets with 1 tablespoon of the oil.

2. Slice off ¼ inch (6 mm) from the bottom of the leeks. Make a shallow, lengthwise slit down one side of each leek, then peel off and discard the outer layer. Carefully separate the remaining layers and wash each piece under cold running water to remove dirt and sand. You should get about 12 good layers from the leeks. Follow the directions for making a calla lily from a leek layer (see Making the Cut on page 23). Create 12 calla lilies. The flowers will curl up a bit at the widest part when baked.

3. If using baby corns, cut them in half lengthwise. If using the orange mini peppers, cut them into 12 narrow triangles that are 2 inches (5 cm) long.

4. Reserve the green trimmings from each layer. Add the lemon juice to the bowl of ice water to keep the greens bright. Add some of the reserved green trimmings to the ice water. They will curl up in 8 to 10 minutes. The longer they stay in the ice bath, the tighter the pieces will curl.

5. Use a paring knife to cut a small X-shaped notch at the base of the flower portion of each calla lily, just above the green part of the stem. You will notice a ridge there; the notch should be just above this ridge. Place the baby corn strips or slivers of orange pepper in each cross-shaped notch so that they are held in place on top of the flowers.

6. Pat the roasted red peppers dry. Cut 3 long strips from the peppers for the ribbon.

7. Move all the vegetables to the unoiled baking sheet, keeping things separate and organized by color and sizes for ease of use during the decorating process. Remove the greens from the ice water and dry them well before placing on the baking sheet.

Oven Preparation

Thirty minutes prior to baking, move the oven rack to the middle and preheat the oven to 450°F (230°C; gas mark 8), allowing time for the oven to come to full temperature.

Shaping and Decorating

1. On the oiled baking sheet, shape your dough while dimpling it (page 17) into a rectangular dough "canvas," about 16 x 11 inches (41 x 28 cm), then coat it with the remaining 2 tablespoons oil.

2. Start by placing the largest leek flower in the center, then place the rest of the calla lilies on the dough, crowding them together into a bouquet as you work. Check that the corn or pepper stamen (center of the flower) is secure as you place each flower.

3. Place the long and curled leaves cut from the green parts of the leeks in and around the flowers.

4. Carefully braid the 3 long red pepper strips and position it around the stems of the bouquet and out to one side to create a flowing ribbon. Trim the flowing ends so that they are neatly slanted.

5. Once you have finished decorating, survey the surface and deflate any large air bubbles with a toothpick or skewer, leaving smaller ones intact (docking). Using piano-style finger motions, gently dimple the dough again. Ultimately, you want to see an uneven bubbly texture, about 1½ to 2 inches (4 to 5 cm) thick in various spots. If the focaccia is flat, allow it to rest for 8 to 10 minutes in a warm, draft-free place.

Baking

1. Just before placing your focaccia in the oven, check the decorations to be sure they are all snug. Secure any that look to be popping off, using a chopstick, skewer, or your fingers.

2. Add finishing salt (if using) and place the focaccia on the middle rack of the oven.

3. Bake for 8 minutes at 450°F (230°C; gas mark 8). Reduce the heat to 375°F (190°C; gas mark 5) and check the decorations again. If any are popping off, coerce them back into the dough by gently and carefully poking down. You don't want to burn yourself. Bake for 10 to 16 more minutes, until the focaccia is golden brown and crisp on the edges.

4. Remove from the oven and let cool for at least 5 to 10 minutes before cutting.

Echinacea

Echinacea, also known as coneflower, is believed to have healing properties for ailments such as the common cold. Layered with chocolate hazelnut filling and garnished with fruit, this focaccia will appeal to the whole family—just what the doctor ordered!

YIELD: 1 FOCACCIA

1 recipe for Sweet Focaccia (page 41)

1 tablespoon neutral oil

8 to 10 large strawberries

6 pitted dark red or orange cherries

1 green pear, peel intact, or kiwi, peeled

2 very firm bananas

Flour, for dusting

¾ cup (225 g) Chocolate Hazelnut Filling (page 166 or store-bought)

Egg wash (1 egg mixed with ¼ cup, or 60 ml, water) or whole milk, for brushing (optional)

Sparkling sugar, for sprinkling (optional)

Special Tools

13 x 8 x 2-inch (33 x 20 x 5 cm) baking dish

Dough Preparation

1. Prepare the dough according to the recipe instructions to when it is chilling in the refrigerator for the last 30 minutes of the second rise.

2. Lightly coat the baking dish with the oil or line with oiled parchment paper. Set aside.

Fruit Preparation

1. Prepare a piece of parchment about the size of your intended focaccia and lay it on an 18 x 13-inch (46 x 33 cm) baking sheet.

2. Remove and discard the strawberry tops, then slice each strawberry in half lengthwise. Place the strawberry halves, cut sides down, and slice lengthwise into ¼-inch-thick (6 mm) slices. These will be the curved flower petals.

3. Slice the cherries in half crosswise. Slice the pear or kiwi lengthwise into 6 to 8 long leaf shapes.

4. Peel the bananas and cut each one in half crosswise. Cut each piece in half lengthwise, then in half lengthwise again, to create 8 stems from each banana.

5. Move all the fruit to the prepared baking sheet, keeping things separate and organized by color and sizes for ease of use during the decorating process.

Shaping and Filling

1. Place the dough on a lightly floured work surface. Use a rolling pin to roll it out to a 21 x 7-inch (53 x 18 cm) rectangle. This dough should be fairly easy to roll out due to the enriched ingredients and not spring back too much. Use a spatula to spread the chocolate hazelnut filling evenly across two-thirds of the dough, leaving an uncoated ½-inch (1 cm) space around the edges.

2. Fold the dough rectangle as if you were folding a letter to go in an envelope. Starting from the end that is not covered with filling, fold inward over the chocolate spread by about 7 inches (18 cm). Next, take the other end that is covered with chocolate and carefully fold over the uncovered layer. You now have a trifold dough full of chocolate hazelnut filling. Use a rolling pin to gently give one or two rolls across the folded dough to secure. Stop rolling if it appears that any chocolate is squeezing out and pinch that end closed.

3. Move the finished dough to the prepared baking dish and, using a toothpick or skewer, poke holes clear through the dough (docking). Don't worry about any chocolate coming through to the top; this will be covered by the lovely strawberry petals and banana stems. This step prevents trapped air from puffing up and creating an uneven bake in the oven.

Oven Preparation

Thirty minutes prior to baking, move the oven rack to the middle and preheat the oven to 350°F (180°C; gas mark 4), allowing time for the oven to come to full temperature.

Decorating

1. Place the banana stems on top of the dough in different directions across the dough, gently pressing them into the dough. Place a cherry half at the top of each stem.

2. Place the strawberry petals, drooping down on either side of the cherries, and place some petals around the top of the cherries. Use tweezers, if necessary, to spread out the petals. Lay the pear or kiwi leaves to fill the space.

3. Once you have finished decorating, let rest, lightly covered with a tea towel, in a warm, draft-free place for 15 to 20 minutes.

Baking

1. If desired, create a shine by brushing the dough with egg wash or whole milk just prior to baking and add a little sparkle, by sprinkling with sparkling sugar.

2. Just before placing your focaccia in the oven, check the decorations to be sure they are all snug. Secure any that look to be popping off, using a chopstick, skewer, or your fingers.

3. Place the focaccia on the middle rack and bake for 25 to 28 minutes, until golden brown, checking the decorations after 8 minutes of baking time. If any decorations are popping off, carefully place them back on and return to oven for the rest of the baking time.

4. Remove from the oven and let cool until warm to the touch before cutting. Any leftovers should be stored in the refrigerator.

Artist Inspired

A year after I made my first bread art, I was gathering flowers from my garden for the dinner table. The flowers were so bright and bold, they reminded me of a Van Gogh painting. I was making bread that day, so I attempted to re-create the vision of this beautiful bouquet, a sunflower focaccia. When I showed my son Gordon, he said, "Wow a real Van Dough you are." I find all types of art to be truly inspiring and easy to translate into bread art, with its vibrant colors and realistic or abstract qualities.

Vincent van Gogh's Irises

Given the lovely complementary colors of irises, it comes as no surprise that Vincent van Gogh painted these flowers as part of his therapeutic healing. So beautiful and flavorful, this focaccia is museum-worthy.

YIELD: 1 FOCACCIA

1 recipe for Basic White Focaccia (page 30) or Basic Whole Wheat Focaccia (page 34)

3 tablespoons extra-virgin olive or neutral oil, divided

1 large oval-shaped red onion

3 orange mini sweet peppers

1 recipe for Quick Pickled Purple Cabbage (page 170)

1 large leek with greens

½ cup (45 g) shredded orange cheddar cheese

1 recipe for Basil Pesto (page 169)

Finishing salt, to taste (optional)

Dough Preparation
Prepare the dough according to the recipe instructions to its second rise.

Vegetable Preparation
1. Prepare two pieces of parchment about the size of your intended focaccia and lay them on two 18 x 13-inch (46 x 33 cm) baking sheets. Coat the parchment on one of the sheets with 1 tablespoon of the oil.

2. Remove and discard the outer layer of the red onion, then slice in half lengthwise. Lay the onion halves, cut sides down, on the cutting board. Using the tip of a paring knife, cut through 3 or 4 layers of onion at a time to create 20 teardrop-shaped petals, about 2 inches (5 cm) wide and 3 inches (7.5 cm) long. They should range in size and colors naturally.

3. Trim the tops of the mini peppers. Cut the peppers in half lengthwise and remove the seeds and pith, then cut each pepper in half lengthwise. Cut out about 12 narrow triangle shapes, 1 to 1½ inches (2.5 to 4 cm) tall, from the halves for the flower stamens (centers).

4. Remove about ¼ cup (30 g) of the quick pickled purple cabbage from the juice and lay it on a paper towel to absorb any extra juices.

5. Cut off the white section of the leek and reserve it for use in other recipes. For the stems, make a slit vertically along the length of the green part of the leek and remove and discard the outer layer. Separate out more layers and wash each piece under cold running water to remove dirt and sand. Use a paring knife to cut each layer into 7 or 8 strips, about 4 inches (10 cm) long and ½ inch (1 cm) wide. Cut 12 oblong shapes from the green part of the leek, 4 to 6 inches (10 to 15 cm) long and 1 inch (2.5 cm) wide at their centers, tapering both ends. These will be the leaves.

6. Move all the vegetables to the unoiled baking sheet, keeping things separate and organized by color and sizes for ease of use during the decorating process. Place the shredded cheese on the baking sheet too.

Oven Preparation

Thirty minutes prior to baking, move the oven rack to the middle and preheat the oven to 450°F (230°C; gas mark 8), allowing time for the oven to come to full temperature.

Shaping and Decorating

1. On the oiled baking sheet, shape the dough while dimpling it (page 17) into an oval that is 15 inches (38 cm) long and 10 to 11 inches (25 to 28 cm) wide, making sure to leave some room on the sides of the baking sheet. Coat the dough with the remaining 2 tablespoons oil, leaving the area where the Basil Pesto will be spread uncoated, then position the baking sheet landscape.

2. Lay a line of leek stems across the middle of the dough, varying the heights as you go. Lay some leek leaves in a similar fashion in among the stems. As you place each stem, "lock" it in place by pushing it down into the dough with a chopstick. To set them in place use the back end of the chopstick to push the stems down into the dough deeply, at the top and bottom and a few spots in between.

3. Spread about ½ cup (120 g) of the basil pesto across the top quarter of the dough and sprinkle shredded cheddar cheese across the bottom half.

4. Place the orange pepper triangles on top of the stems for the flower centers.

5. Lay out the pickled cabbage pieces, wrapping them around and up the orange centers.

6. Position the onion petals on either side of the cabbage, with the petals drooping downward, to complete each flower.

7. Once you have finished decorating, survey the surface and deflate any large air bubbles with a toothpick or skewer, leaving smaller ones intact (docking). Using piano-style finger motions, gently dimple the dough again. Ultimately, you want to see an uneven bubbly texture, about 1½ to 2 inches (4 to 5 cm) thick in various spots. If the focaccia is flat, allow it to rest for 8 to 10 minutes in a warm, draft-free place.

Baking

1. Just before placing your focaccia in the oven, check the decorations to be sure they are all snug. Secure any that look to be popping off, using the chopstick, a skewer, or your fingers.

2. Add finishing salt (if using) and place the focaccia on the middle rack of the oven.

3. Bake for 8 minutes at 450°F (230°C; gas mark 8). Reduce the heat to 375°F (190°C; gas mark 5) and check the decorations again. If any are popping off, coerce them back into the dough by gently and carefully poking down. You don't want to burn yourself. Bake for 10 to 16 more minutes, until the focaccia is golden brown and crisp on the edges.

4. Remove from the oven and let cool for at least 5 to 10 minutes before cutting.

Georgia O'Keeffe's Open Flower

When cutting a red onion in half, it's easy to see the inspiration for this beautiful focaccia, one of Georgia O'Keeffe's wonderful flower paintings.

YIELD: 2 SQUARE FOCACCIA

1 recipe for Basic White Focaccia (page 30) or Basic Whole Wheat Focaccia (page 34)

6 tablespoons extra-virgin olive or neutral oil, divided

1 teaspoon lemon juice

Bowl of ice water

12 leaves arugula

2 large oval-shaped red onions

4 orange mini sweet peppers

Finishing salt, to taste (optional)

Dough Preparation

Prepare the dough according to the recipe instructions to its second rise.

Vegetable Preparation

1. Prepare three pieces of parchment about the size of your intended focaccia and lay them on three 18 x 13-inch (46 x 33 cm) baking sheets. Coat the parchment on two of the sheets with 1 tablespoon of oil each.

2. Add the lemon juice to the bowl of ice water to keep the greens bright. Place the arugula in the bowl of ice water.

3. Remove and discard the outer layer from the red onion. Slice the onion into ¼-inch-thick (6 mm) slices. Separate the slices so that each is 2 layers thick. If needed, cut the root area off to allow for easier separating. You should get about 8 slices from the onion, and the slices should end up being a mix of oval shapes with pointed tops and rounder shapes.

4. Trim the tops of the mini peppers. Cut the peppers in half lengthwise and remove the seeds and pith, then cut each pepper half lengthwise. Cut out about 40 triangle shapes that are 2 inches (5 cm) long and ¼ inch (6 mm) wide.

5. Move all the vegetables to the unoiled baking sheet, keeping things separate and organized by color and sizes for ease of use during the decorating process. Remove the greens from the ice water and dry them well before placing on the baking sheet.

Oven Preparation

Thirty minutes prior to baking, move the oven racks to the middle and lower rungs and preheat the oven to 450°F (230°C; gas mark 8), allowing time for the oven to come to full temperature.

Shaping

1. Use a bowl scraper to divide the dough evenly in half and set one half aside. Lay the other half in the center of one of the oiled baking sheets.

2. Shape the dough while dimpling it (page 17) into an 8-inch (20 cm) square, then coat it with 2 tablespoons of the oil. Repeat shaping and dimpling the other piece of dough into a square on the second oiled baking sheet, then coat it with the remaining 2 tablespoons oil. If the dough is springing back, allow it to rest for 5 to 8 minutes. The dough will then be supple and ready for shaping again.

Decorating

1. Position one of the sheets so that the square is a diamond shape. Begin by placing a round piece of onion at the bottom corner of the square. Lay the largest oval petal above the round piece, then continue placing oval petals working upward and outward across the surface. Work from the largest petals across the center, graduating to smaller petals toward the outer edges of the dough. Place an orange pepper triangle in the middle of each petal. Lay the arugula leaves along the bottom edges leading out from the original round onion piece.

2. Repeat the design on the second square of dough.

3. Once you have finished decorating, survey the surface and deflate any large air bubbles with a toothpick or skewer, leaving smaller ones intact (docking). Using piano-style finger motions, gently dimple the dough again. Ultimately, you want to see an uneven bubbly texture, about 1½ to 2 inches (4 to 5 cm) thick in various spots. If the focaccia is flat, allow it to rest for 8 to 10 minutes in a warm, draft-free place.

Baking

1. Just before placing your focaccia in the oven, check the decorations to be sure they are all snug. Secure any that look to be popping off, using a chopstick, skewer, or your fingers.

2. Add finishing salt (if using) and place the focaccia on the middle and lower racks of the oven.

3. Bake for 10 minutes at 450°F (230°C; gas mark 8). Reduce the heat to 375°F (190°C; gas mark 5) and check the decorations again. If any are popping off, coerce them back into the dough by gently and carefully poking down. You don't want to burn yourself. Swap the baking sheets over and bake for 8 to 12 more minutes, until both focaccia are golden brown and crisp on the edges.

4. Remove from the oven and let cool for at least 5 to 10 minutes before cutting.

Takashi Murakami's Happy Flowers

Takashi Murakami's colorful, smiling flowers are guaranteed to brighten anyone's day. This is the perfect project to express your inner artist!

YIELD: 1 FOCACCIA

1 recipe for Basic White Focaccia (page 30) or Basic Whole Wheat Focaccia (page 34)

3 tablespoons extra-virgin olive or neutral oil, divided

1 large red onion

1 yellow mini sweet bell pepper

1 orange mini sweet bell pepper

1 small zucchini

1 small yellow squash

1 large whole roasted red pepper (see page 25 for how to roast your own)

1 large orange carrot, peeled

1 large red carrot, peeled

1 large leek with greens

12 to 16 peppercorns

Finishing salt, to taste (optional)

Special Tools

Small, medium, and large flower-shaped cookie cutters

Mini half-circle and circle cookie cutters

Dough Preparation

Prepare the dough according to the recipe instructions to its second rise.

Vegetable Preparation

1. Prepare two pieces of parchment about the size of your intended focaccia and lay them on two 18 x 13-inch (46 x 33 cm) baking sheets. Coat the parchment on one of the sheets with 1 tablespoon of the oil.

2. Prep the red onion and mini peppers for cutting out shapes (see Making the Cut on pages 23 and 24).

3. Cut the zucchini and yellow squash into ½-inch-thick (1 cm) slices for cutting.

4. Cut the roasted pepper into 2 strips that are 3 inches (7.5 cm) long and ¼ inch (6 mm) wide.

5. Use the flower cookie cutters to cut flower shapes out of the zucchini, yellow squash, red onion, mini peppers, and roasted red pepper. Cut out 2 or 3 shapes of

every size in each of the different colored vegetables. Use the mini circle cutter to cut out circles from a few different colored vegetables. Also, cut out the centers from the zucchini and yellow squash with a smaller flower cookie cutter and fill them with a flower of the same size in a contrasting color.

6. Use a julienne peeler to slice about ten 3-inch-long (7.5 cm) strips from both carrots.

7. Slice the leek greens into strips that are 3 inches (7.5 cm) long and ¼ inch (6 mm) wide.

8. Poach the carrot and leek into about 12 strips in 4 cups (960 ml) of boiling water for 2 minutes to create some flexibility. (Turn off the heat and let the boiling water settle for 2 minutes before adding the vegetables.)

9. Poke 2 holes in the larger flowers and push the peppercorns into the holes for eyes. Cut half circles in these same flowers for mouths using the half-circle cutter. Fill the spaces with contrasting-color smiles or leave open for the dough to show through.

10. Move all the vegetables to the unoiled baking sheet, keeping things separate and organized by color and sizes for ease of use during the decorating process. Pat dry the carrot and leek strips before placing on the baking sheet.

Oven Preparation

Thirty minutes prior to baking, move the oven rack to the middle and preheat the oven to 450°F (230°C; gas mark 8), allowing time for the oven to come to full temperature.

Shaping and Decorating

1. On the oiled baking sheet, shape your dough while dimpling it (page 17) into a rectangular dough "canvas," about 16 x 11 inches (41 x 28 cm), then coat it with the remaining 2 tablespoons oil.

2. Begin by placing the large flowers on the dough. Create large flowers from the leek and carrot strips by bending and curving the strips for petals. Place mini circles in contrasting colors as the centers. Also make a large flower with the roasted red pepper strips and place a mini star as its center.

3. Start adding other flowers in various sizes and colors around the large flowers, covering the surface of the dough. Add the flower faces at different angles to add personality.

4. Once you have finished decorating, survey the surface and deflate any large air bubbles with a toothpick or skewer, leaving smaller ones intact (docking). Using piano-style finger motions, gently dimple the dough again. Ultimately, you want to see an uneven bubbly texture, about 1½ to 2 inches (4 to 5 cm) thick in various spots. If the focaccia is flat, allow it to rest for 8 to 10 minutes in a warm, draft-free place.

Baking

1. Just before placing your focaccia in the oven, check the decorations to be sure they are all snug. Secure any that look to be popping off, using the chopstick or your fingers.

2. Add finishing salt (if using) and place the focaccia on the middle rack of the oven.

3. Bake for 8 minutes at 450°F (230°C; gas mark 8). Reduce the heat to 375°F (190°C; gas mark 5) and check the decorations again. If any are popping off, coerce them back into the dough by gently and carefully poking down. You don't want to burn yourself. Bake for 10 to 16 more minutes, until the focaccia is golden brown and crisp on the edges.

4. Remove from the oven and let cool for at least 5 to 10 minutes before cutting.

Pablo Picasso's Faces

There is no mistaking a Picasso. And a word of advice: Any time some not-so-perfect bread art comes out of the kitchen, just say, "It's a Picasso," no matter if things are sliding or popping off. Works every time!

YIELD: 1 FOCACCIA

1 recipe for Basic White Focaccia (page 30) or Basic Whole Wheat Focaccia (page 34)

3 tablespoons extra-virgin olive or neutral oil, divided

1 teaspoon lemon juice

Bowl of ice water

6 leaves basil

3 or 4 sprigs flat-leaf parsley

1 eggplant

1 small red onion

2 pitted black olives

¼ cup (40 g) finely chopped pitted kalamata olives

1 teaspoon chopped fresh rosemary

6 whole artichoke hearts, from a can or jar

1 large orange carrot, peeled

1 recipe for Basil Pesto (page 169)

Finishing salt, to taste

Dough Preparation

Prepare the dough according to the recipe instructions to its second rise.

Vegetable Preparation

1. Prepare two pieces of parchment about the size of your intended focaccia and lay them on two 18 x 13-inch (46 x 33 cm) baking sheets. Coat the parchment on one of the sheets with 1 tablespoon of the oil.

2. Add the lemon juice to the bowl of ice water to keep the greens bright. Place the basil and parsley in the ice water.

3. Carefully peel the eggplant lengthwise into long pieces, reserving the peel for the facial features. Cut the peel into 14 long strips about ¼ inch (6 mm) wide, then use a paring knife to cut the following shapes from a few of the strips: a 7- to 9-inch (18 to 23 cm) zigzag strip for the combined nose and mouth; 2 shorter, thicker strips for the ears; and 8 short, very thin strips for the eyes and eyebrows. Cut a trapezoid-shaped piece from the eggplant flesh that is 2 to 2½ inches (5 to 6 cm) tall and ¼ inch (6 mm) thick, with the top side being 1½ inches (4 cm) long and the bottom side being 2 inches (5 cm) long.

4. Cut the red onion into 3 oblong shapes about 3 inches (7.5 cm) long and ½ inch (6 mm) wide. Also finely chop some onion to get 3 tablespoons.

5. Pat the black olives dry. Cut them in half lengthwise for the pupils.

6. In a small bowl, stir together the chopped kalamata olives and chopped onion with the rosemary.

7. Finely chop the artichokes and shred the carrot.

8. Remove the basil from the ice water, dry well, and cut chiffonade-style.

9. Move all the vegetables to the unoiled baking sheet, keeping things separate and organized by color and sizes for ease of use during the decorating process. Remove the parsley from the ice water and dry well before placing on the baking sheet.

Oven Preparation

Thirty minutes prior to baking, move the oven rack to the middle and preheat the oven to 450°F (230°C; gas mark 8), allowing time for the oven to come to full temperature.

Shaping and Decorating

1. On the oiled baking sheet, shape the dough while dimpling it (page 17) into an oval that is 16 inches (41 cm) long and 10 inches (25 cm) wide, making sure to leave some room on the sides of the baking sheet. Coat the dough with the remaining 2 tablespoons oil, leaving the area where the Basil Pesto will be spread uncoated.

2. Outline the entire focaccia with the long eggplant strips, then make an inner oval for the face outline, leaving space for the ears. Place 2 strips vertically, about 2 inches (5 cm) apart, to define the neck. As you place each item, "lock" it in place by pushing it down into the dough with a chopstick. To set them in place use the back end of the chopstick to push the eggplant down into the dough deeply, at the top and bottom and a few spots in between.

3. Use the trapezoid-shaped piece of eggplant to fit inside the neck area.

4. Spread the pesto on the left side from the base of the neck, around the outside edge of the dough, and up to the top middle. Sprinkle the basil strips on top of the pesto.

5. Spread some of the chopped kalamata olive mixture on the right side from the base of the neck, around the outside edge of the dough, and up to the top middle. Scatter some shredded carrot over the olives.

6. Place the chopped artichoke hearts on the left half of the inner oval and the remaining shredded carrots on the right half.

7. Place the eggplant pieces for the ears, curving them in a C shape facing outward. Place 2 black olive halves inside the ears.

8. Create the outlines of the eyes with the very thin strips of eggplant and the remaining 2 black olive halves for the pupils. Place the remaining thin strips over the eyes for the eyebrows, slightly curving them.

9. Lay the zigzag piece a little off center to the left for the nose and mouth, starting below the left eye. Lay the 2 slices of red onion down the entire face, skewing a little to the right under the right eye.

10. Fill in the space between the zigzag piece and the red onion with the remaining chopped kalamata olive mixture.

11. Once you have finished decorating, survey the surface and deflate any large air bubbles with a toothpick or skewer, leaving smaller ones intact (docking). Using piano-style finger motions, gently dimple the dough again. Ultimately, you want to see an uneven bubbly texture, about 1½ to 2 inches (4 to 5 cm) thick in various spots. If the focaccia is flat, allow it to rest for 8 to 10 minutes in a warm, draft-free place.

Baking

1. Just before placing your focaccia in the oven, check the decorations to be sure they are all snug. Secure any that look to be popping off, using the chopstick, a skewer, or your fingers.

2. Add finishing salt (if using) and place the focaccia on the middle rack of the oven.

3. Bake for 8 minutes at 450°F (230°C; gas mark 8). Reduce the heat to 375°F (190°C; gas mark 5) and check the decorations again. If any are popping off, coerce them back into the dough by gently and carefully poking down. You don't want to burn yourself. Bake for 10 to 16 more minutes, until the focaccia is golden brown and crisp on the edges.

4. Remove from the oven and let cool for at least 5 to 10 minutes before cutting.

Wassily Kandinsky's Circles in Squares

Wassily Kandinsky was an Expressionist artist, using color, lines, and shapes to convey thought and emotion. Using concentric circles with color variations and lines, this style can be easily replicated with colorful vegetables for a whimsical focaccia that's fun to make.

YIELD: 1 FOCACCIA

1 recipe for Basic White Focaccia (page 30) or Basic Whole Wheat Focaccia (page 34)

3 tablespoons extra-virgin olive or neutral oil, divided

1 large red bell pepper

1 large yellow bell pepper

1 large orange bell pepper

1 large green bell pepper

1 large red onion

1 small jalapeño pepper

2 pitted black olives

Smoked paprika, to taste (optional)

Dough Preparation

Prepare the dough according to the recipe instructions to its second rise.

Vegetable Preparation

1. Prepare two pieces of parchment about the size of your intended focaccia and lay them on two 18 x 13-inch (46 x 33 cm) baking sheets. Coat the parchment on one of the sheets with 1 tablespoon of the oil.

2. Make 16 to 18 circles in a variety of sizes and colors from all the vegetables. Remove the stem, seeds, and cores from the bell and jalapeño peppers, then cut into ¼-inch-thick (6 mm) rings. Also slice the red onion crosswise into ¼-inch-thick (6 mm) rings.

3. Cut any leftover pieces of peppers and onion into ¼-inch (6 mm) squares.

4. Pat the olives dry. Cut them in half crosswise.

5. Move all the vegetables to the unoiled baking sheet, keeping things separate and organized by color and sizes for ease of use during the decorating process.

Oven Preparation

Thirty minutes prior to baking, move the oven rack to the middle and preheat the oven to 450°F (230°C; gas mark 8), allowing time for the oven to come to full temperature.

Shaping and Decorating

1. On the oiled baking sheet, shape your dough while dimpling it (page 17) into a rectangular dough "canvas," about 16 x 11 inches (41 x 28 cm), then coat it with the remaining 2 tablespoons oil.

2. If using, lightly sprinkle the dough with the smoked paprika to give it both color and a smoky flavor.

3. Begin by laying the largest ring pieces on the dough, four down and two across.

4. Place smaller circles in contrasting colors inside the large circles.

5. Continue to fill the circles using different colors.

6. Fill in the empty spaces around the circles with the cut squares, covering the entire dough.

7. Once you have finished decorating, survey the surface and deflate any large air bubbles with a toothpick or skewer, leaving smaller ones intact (docking). Using piano-style finger motions, gently dimple the dough again. Ultimately, you want to see an uneven bubbly texture, about 1½ to 2 inches (4 to 5 cm) thick in various spots. If the focaccia is flat, allow it to rest for 8 to 10 minutes in a warm, draft-free place.

Baking

1. Just before placing your focaccia in the oven, check the decorations to be sure they are all snug. Secure any that look to be popping off, using a chopstick, skewer, or your fingers.

2. Add finishing salt (if using) and place the focaccia on the middle rack of the oven.

3. Bake for 8 minutes at 450°F (230°C; gas mark 8). Reduce the heat to 375°F (190°C; gas mark 5) and check the decorations again. If any are popping off, coerce them back into the dough by gently and carefully poking down. You don't want to burn yourself. Bake for 10 to 16 more minutes, until the focaccia is golden brown and crisp on the edges.

4. Remove from the oven and let cool for at least 5 to 10 minutes before cutting.

Claude Monet's Lily Pond

Did you know Monet was meticulous about hosting dinner parties? So, let this Impressionist bread art make an impression on your guests.

YIELD: 1 FOCACCIA

1 recipe for Basic White Focaccia (page 30) or Basic Whole Wheat Focaccia (page 34)

2 tablespoons extra-virgin olive or neutral oil, divided

1 small or medium green bell pepper

1 large red onion

Bowl of ice water

1 orange mini sweet pepper

6 pitted kalamata olives

2 scallions

½ cup (60 g) crumbled feta cheese

2 tablespoons capers, rinsed

1 tablespoon black and white sesame seeds

1 recipe for Basil Pesto (page 169)

Finishing salt, to taste (optional)

Dough Preparation

Prepare the dough according to the recipe instructions to its second rise.

Vegetable Preparation

1. Prepare two pieces of parchment about the size of your intended focaccia and lay them on two 18 x 13-inch (46 x 33 cm) baking sheets. Coat the parchment on one of the sheets with 1 tablespoon of the oil.

2. Remove the stem, seeds, and pith from the green pepper, then cut it into five ¼-inch-thick (6 mm) rings. Cut the rings in half to create 10 half circles. Cut 4 of those in half again to make even smaller half circles.

3. Remove and discard the outer layer of the red onion. Separate out more layers, then cut out eighteen 1-inch-tall (2.5 cm) triangles. Fray the wide end of each triangle by laying each one flat on a cutting board and using a paring knife to gently make 3 vertical slits without cutting all the way through. Place the frayed onions in the bowl of ice water to encourage them to open up slightly. Also cut 3 strips from the onion, each ¼ inch (6 mm) wide and 5 inches (12.5 cm) long.

4. Slice the orange mini pepper into 6 thin sticks 3 inches (7.5 cm) long. Pat the olives dry, then slice them in half lengthwise. Fray them by laying the olive halves, cut sides down, on a cutting board and using a paring knife to make 3 vertical slits in each half, leaving one end intact.

5. Cut off ½ inch (6 mm) from the bottom of each scallion, then cut one scallion into a length of 5 to 6 inches (12.5 to 15 cm) and the other one into a 3-inch (7.5 cm) length, making sure both pieces have green on top and white on the bottom. Lay the pieces on a cutting board and run a paring knife down the entire length of the longer one to fray it into a few pieces. Fray only the green part of the shorter one, leaving ½ inch (6 mm) of the bottom intact. Place the frayed scallions in the ice water to open them up.

6. Move all the vegetables to the unoiled baking sheet, keeping things separate and organized by color and sizes for ease of use during the decorating process. Place the crumbled cheese, capers, and sesame seeds on the baking sheet too.

Oven Preparation

Thirty minutes prior to baking, move the oven rack to the middle and preheat the oven to 450°F (230°C; gas mark 8), allowing time for the oven to come to full temperature.

Shaping and Decorating

1. On the oiled baking sheet, shape your dough while dimpling it (page 17) into a rectangular dough "canvas," about 16 x 11 inches (41 x 28 cm), then coat it with the remaining 1 tablespoon oil, leaving the areas where the Basil Pesto will be spread uncoated.

2. Starting at the bottom of the dough, place the green peppers as a cluster of lily pads, with the larger pieces at the bottom and the smaller ones at the top. Place a teaspoon of pesto in each one. Place the frayed onions as flowers in between and around the lily pads.

3. Build the bridge by vertically laying the 6 orange pepper sticks in an arch in the middle of the dough. Lay the long onion strips horizontally across the pepper sticks, following the natural curve of the strips for the bridge shape. Create bush-like plants with the frayed olives around the base of the bridge on either side. Spread the olive pieces open as you push them down slightly into the dough to help the pieces stay spread apart.

4. Place the longer frayed pieces of scallion with the white ends at the top on the left side of the bridge, spreading them out and creating a drooping-willow effect by bending the scallions downward. Place the shorter frayed scallion on the right side of the bridge, spreading a teaspoon of pesto above it. As you place each item, "lock" it in place by pushing it down into the dough with a chopstick. To set them in place use the back end of the chopstick to push the stems down into the dough deeply, at the top and bottom and a few spots in between. Scatter the feta cheese and capers on and around the drooping-willow scallions. Sprinkle the black and white sesame seeds around the bottom of the dough.

5. Once you have finished decorating, survey the surface and deflate any large air bubbles with a toothpick or skewer, leaving smaller ones intact (docking). Using piano-style finger motions, gently dimple the dough again. Ultimately, you want to see an uneven bubbly texture, about 1½ to 2 inches (4 to 5 cm) thick in various spots. If the focaccia is flat, allow it to rest for 8 to 10 minutes in a warm, draft-free place.

Baking

1. Just before placing your focaccia in the oven, check the decorations to be sure they are all snug. Secure any that look to be popping off, using the chopstick, a skewer, or your fingers.

2. Add finishing salt (if using) and place the focaccia on the middle rack of the oven.

3. Bake for 8 minutes at 450°F (230°C; gas mark 8). Reduce the heat to 375°F (190°C; gas mark 5) and check the decorations again. If any are popping off, coerce them back into the dough by gently and carefully poking down. You don't want to burn yourself. Bake for 10 to 16 more minutes, until the focaccia is golden brown and crisp on the edges.

4. Remove from the oven and let cool for at least 5 to 10 minutes before cutting.

Alma Thomas' Brushstrokes of Color

Alma Thomas didn't create her signature abstract paintings, described as being made up of "micro-units of color" by the Museum of Modern Art, until she was in her seventies. It is amazing how many different colors there are in vegetables and how easy it is to replicate this colorful design.

YIELD: 1 FOCACCIA

1 recipe for Basic White Focaccia (page 30) or Basic Whole Wheat Focaccia (page 34)

3 tablespoons extra-virgin olive or neutral oil, divided

1 large red bell pepper

1 large yellow bell pepper

1 large orange bell pepper

1 large red onion

1 large leek, green part only

15 pitted black olives

1 large purple carrot (or purple potato or Japanese sweet potato), peeled

Finishing salt, to taste (optional)

Dough Preparation

Prepare the dough according to the recipe instructions to its second rise.

Vegetable Preparation

1. Prepare two pieces of parchment about the size of your intended focaccia and lay them on two 18 x 13-inch (46 x 33 cm) baking sheets. Coat the parchment on one of the sheets with 1 tablespoon of the oil.

2. Cut all the vegetables into small rectangular pieces, about ¼ x ⅓ inch (5 x 8 mm). These can be random and slightly longer or shorter on some pieces; the idea is to create random brushstrokes.

3. Move all the vegetables to the unoiled bakink sheet, keeping things separate and organized by color and sizes for ease of use during the decorating process.

Oven Preparation

Thirty minutes prior to baking, move the oven rack to the middle and preheat the oven to 450°F (230°C; gas mark 8), allowing time for the oven to come to full temperature.

Shaping and Decorating

1. On the oiled baking sheet, shape your dough while dimpling it (page 17) into a

rectangular dough "canvas," about 16 x 11 inches (41 x 28 cm), then coat the dough with the remaining 2 tablespoons oil. Position the baking sheet landscape so that you are working along the dough in horizontal stripes.

2. First, create the green mountain in the center with the green leek, then work upward, following the color pattern of yellow, orange, red, and a mixture of orange and yellow on top. Now, move below the green line, following the color pattern of light to dark purples. Be sure to press the vegetables slightly down into the dough.

3. Once you have finished decorating, survey the surface and deflate any large air bubbles with a toothpick or skewer, leaving smaller ones intact (docking). Using piano-style finger motions, gently dimple the dough again. Ultimately, you want to see an uneven bubbly texture, about 1½ to 2 inches (4 to 5 cm) thick in various spots. If the focaccia is flat, allow it to rest for 8 to 10 minutes in a warm, draft-free place.

Baking

1. Just before placing your focaccia in the oven, check the decorations to be sure they are all snug. Secure any that look to be popping off, using a chopstick, skewer, or your fingers.

2. Add finishing salt (if using) and place the focaccia on the middle rack of the oven.

3. Bake for 8 minutes at 450°F (230°C; gas mark 8). Reduce the heat to 375°F (190°C; gas mark 5) and check the decorations again. If any are popping off, coerce them back into the dough by gently and carefully poking down. You don't want to burn yourself. Bake for 10 to 16 more minutes, until the focaccia is golden brown and crisp on the edges.

4. Remove from the oven and let cool for at least 5 to 10 minutes before cutting.

Nature Inspired

The focaccia projects in this section are reflections of the beauty found in nature. When taking a walk or a hike, you can find inspiration everywhere. I found inspiration in the twisting branches of scrub oaks and the grain in knotty pines; a picnic at the beach that revealed a variety of gifts from the sea, strewn over the sand and adorned on sandcastles; and the most fabulous autumn colors that beckoned as fallen leaves along tree-lined paths.

Fall Leaves

I live in New England. Autumn is always a favorite time of year, as the leaves change colors. Those who make the journey to see the leaves are affectionately called "leaf peepers." This focaccia would be a lovely snack on any leaf-peeping adventure.

YIELD: 1 FOCACCIA

1 recipe for Basic White Focaccia (page 30) or Basic Whole Wheat Focaccia (page 34)

1 tablespoon plus 2 teaspoons extra-virgin olive or neutral oil, divided

1 teaspoon lemon juice

Bowl of ice water

12 chives

2 sprigs parsley

2 red mini sweet peppers

2 yellow mini sweet peppers

2 orange mini sweet peppers

Flour, for dusting

Finishing salt, to taste (optional)

Special Tools

Leaf-shaped cookie cutters

Dough Preparation

Prepare the dough according to the recipe instructions to its second rise.

Vegetable Preparation

1. Prepare two pieces of parchment about the size of your intended focaccia and lay them on two 18 x 13-inch (46 x 33 cm) baking sheets. Coat the parchment on one of the baking sheets with 1 tablespoon of the oil.

2. Add the lemon juice to the bowl of ice water to keep the greens bright. Trim the chives and place them in the ice water with the parsley.

3. Trim the tops of the mini peppers. Cut the peppers in half lengthwise and remove the seeds and pith, then cut each pepper half lengthwise. Mince each pepper half and place in separate piles by color on the unoiled baking sheet.

4. Remove the greens from the ice water and dry them well before placing on the baking sheet.

Oven Preparation

Thirty minutes prior to baking, move the oven rack to the middle and preheat the oven to 450°F (230°C; gas mark 8), allowing time for the oven to come to full temperature.

Shaping

1. Place the dough on a lightly floured surface. Cut off one-third of the dough and set aside.

2. Place the larger piece of dough on the oiled baking sheet and shape while dimpling it (page 17) into a 10 x 6-inch (25 x 15 cm) rectangle. This is your base dough. Coat the dough with 1 teaspoon of the oil and set aside.

3. Using a rolling pin, roll out the smaller piece of dough to the same size as the larger piece. Move the dough to a piece of parchment paper and dust the surface with flour.

4. Use the cookie cutters to randomly cut out leaf shapes all over the surface of the dough and carefully remove the cutout shapes. Aim for around 8 to 10 cutouts across the surface. This is your top dough.

Decorating

1. Carefully flip the parchment paper with the top dough on onto the base dough. Gently press to adhere and adjust so that the dough corners match up.

2. Fill each leaf cutout with minced peppers. Mix up some of the colors to create multicolored leaves too. Once all the leaf cutouts are filled, pull off the smaller sprigs of parsley from the larger sprigs and scatter around the cutouts to complete the design. Coat the top of the focaccia with the remaining 1 teaspoon oil..

3. Place the chives around the design.

4. Allow the dough to rise, covered, in a warm, draft-free place for another 15 minutes.

5. You will need to dock (page 17) this dough to be sure no irregular puffing up happens during the bake. Survey the surface and deflate any large air bubbles with a toothpick or skewer, leaving smaller ones intact. Be sure to poke all the way down, remembering that this focaccia is in 2 layers.

Baking

1. Just before placing your focaccia in the oven, check the decorations to be sure they are all snug. Secure any that look to be popping off, using a chopstick, skewer, or your fingers.

2. Add finishing salt (if using) and place the focaccia on the middle rack of the oven.

3. Bake for 8 minutes at 450°F (230°C; gas mark 8). Reduce the heat to 375°F (190°C; gas mark 5) and check the decorations again. If any are popping off, coerce them back into the dough by gently and carefully poking down. You don't want to burn yourself. Bake for 10 to 16 more minutes, until the focaccia is golden brown and crisp on the edges.

4. Remove from the oven and let cool for at least 5 to 10 minutes before cutting.

Under the Sea

With so many colors and shapes found in the ocean and on the beach, you can easily replicate the underwater scene of your imagination with this whimsical focaccia while looking forward to the warm days of summer.

YIELD: 1 FOCACCIA

1 recipe for Basic White Focaccia (page 30) or Basic Whole Wheat Focaccia (page 34)

3 tablespoons extra-virgin olive or neutral oil, divided

1 teaspoon lemon juice

Bowl of ice water

6 leaves arugula

1 sprig dill

4 large leaves basil

3 scallions

1 small shallot

2 cloves garlic

4 pitted kalamata olives

1 large purple carrot (preferably with an orange center), peeled

1 tablespoon capers, rinsed

¼ cup (30 g) crumbled feta or goat cheese

1 tablespoon white sesame seeds or golden flaxseeds

1 sprig rosemary

Finishing salt, to taste (optional)

Special Tools

Mini fish-shaped cookie cutter (optional)

Dough Preparation

Prepare the dough according to the recipe instructions to its second rise.

Vegetable Preparation

1. Prepare two pieces of parchment about the size of your intended focaccia and lay them on two 18 x 13-inch (46 x 33 cm) baking sheets. Coat the parchment on one of the baking sheets with 1 tablespoon of the oil.

2. Add the lemon juice to the bowl of ice water to keep the greens bright. Place the arugula, dill, and basil in the ice water.

3. Lay the scallions flat and cut 1 inch (2.5 cm) from both the tops and bottoms. Cut several thin slices along the bias and place in the ice water to curl up for seaweed.

4. Peel the shallot and cut into ¼-inch-thick (6 mm) slices for seashells. Cut the garlic cloves into thin slices lengthwise, also for seashells.

5. Pat the olives dry. Cut them in half lengthwise.

6. Cut the purple carrot into ¼-inch-thick (6 mm) rounds and use the cookie cutter to cut out 7 or 8 fish. If you don't have a fish cutter, you can cut them freehand with a paring knife by cutting out a small oval shape with a fish tail on one end. With the remaining part of the carrot, use a julienne peeler to cut slices for seaweed.

7. Move all the vegetables to the unoiled baking sheet, keeping things separate and organized by color and sizes for ease of use during the decorating process. Remove the greens from the ice water and dry them well before placing on the baking sheet. Place the capers, crumbled cheese, seeds, and rosemary on the baking sheet too.

Oven Preparation

Thirty minutes prior to baking, move the oven rack to the middle and preheat the oven to 450°F (230°C; gas mark 8), allowing time for the oven to come to full temperature.

Shaping and Decorating

1. On the oiled baking sheet, shape your dough while dimpling it (page 17) into a rectangular dough "canvas," about 16 x 11 inches (41 x 28 cm), then coat the dough with the remaining 2 tablespoons oil. Position the baking sheet landscape.

2. Arrange the arugula and scallions as tall sea plants on the right and left sides of the dough. As you place each sea plant, "lock" it in place by pushing it down into the dough with a chopstick. To set them in place use the back end of the chopstick to push the stems down into the dough deeply, at the top and bottom and a few spots in between. The dill and rosemary needles can be used as leaves on one of the scallions.

3. Place 10 to 12 capers on either side of some of the scallion greens.

4. Create a couple of purple seaweed plants with the purple carrot slices. Lay out the kalamata olive, shallot, and garlic slices in pairs along the bottom of the dough to decorate the floor of the ocean.

5. Place the fish in and around the greens so that they look like they are swimming among the seaweed.

6. Sprinkle the sesame seeds or golden flaxseeds around the bottom of the dough to highlight the ocean floor, and then sprinkle the crumbled feta along the bottom and top edges of the dough.

7. Cut the basil using a chiffonade cut, then sprinkle across the top and bottom of the dough.

8. Once you have finished decorating, survey the surface and deflate any large air bubbles with a toothpick or skewer, leaving smaller ones intact (docking). Using piano-style finger motions, gently dimple the dough again. Ultimately, you want to see an uneven bubbly texture, about 1½ to 2 inches (4 to 5 cm) thick in various spots. If the focaccia is flat, allow it to rest for 8 to 10 minutes in a warm, draft-free place.

Baking

1. Just before placing your focaccia in the oven, check the decorations to be sure they are all snug. Secure any that look to be popping off, using the chopstick, a skewer, or your fingers.

2. Add finishing salt (if using) and place the focaccia on the middle rack of the oven.

3. Bake for 8 minutes at 450°F (230°C; gas mark 8). Reduce the heat to 375°F (190°C; gas mark 5) and check the decorations again. If any are popping off, coerce them back into the dough by gently and carefully poking down. You don't want to burn yourself. Bake for 10 to 16 more minutes, until the focaccia is golden brown and crisp on the edges.

4. Remove from the oven and let cool for at least 5 to 10 minutes before cutting.

Tree of Life

The Tree of Life is represented in mythology, philosophy, and religion. For this focaccia, the branches and roots hold tiny, colorful flowers, reminding us of how much variety of life there is on our lovely planet, including us.

YIELD: 1 FOCACCIA

1 recipe for Basic White Focaccia (page 30) or Basic Whole Wheat Focaccia (page 34)

1 tablespoon dark cocoa powder

3 tablespoons extra-virgin olive or neutral oil, divided

1 teaspoon lemon juice

Bowl of ice water

4 to 6 small leaves sage

4 to 6 small leaves basil

2 red mini sweet peppers

2 yellow mini sweet peppers

2 orange mini sweet peppers

1 small red onion

1 scallion

2 pitted black olives

1 tablespoon capers, rinsed

1 sprig rosemary

Flour, for dusting

Finishing salt, to taste (optional)

Special Tools

Mini flower-shaped cookie cutters

Dough Preparation

1. Prepare the dough according to the recipe instructions to right before the first set of stretch and folds. Cut off a portion of dough about the size of a lemon.

2. Sprinkle the dark cocoa powder on the work surface and work this small portion of dough until all the cocoa is incorporated. This will be the tree.

3. Continue with the recipe as instructed for both doughs, stretching and folding this smaller piece only 5 or 6 times before its second rise.

Vegetable Preparation

1. Prepare two pieces of parchment about the size of your intended focaccia and lay them on two 18 x 13-inch (46 x 33 cm) baking sheets. Coat the parchment on one of the sheets with 1 tablespoon of the oil.

2. Add the lemon juice to the bowl of ice water to keep the greens bright. Place the sage and basil leaves in the ice water.

3. Prep the peppers for cutting out shapes (see Making the Cut on page 23). Use the cookie cutters to cut out 20 to 24 small flowers.

4. Remove and discard the outer layer of the red onion and cut in half. Separate out 3 or 4 layers together and use the cookie cutters to cut out some flowers.

5. Make 8 scallion stems about 1 inch (2.5 cm) long and ¼ inch (6 mm) wide. Cut 12 small leaf shapes from the green part of the scallion.

6. Pat the olives dry. Cut 1 olive into 4 rings, then cut the remaining olive in half lengthwise and each half in half crosswise.

7. Move all the vegetables to the unoiled baking sheet, keeping things separate and organized by color and sizes for ease of use during the decorating process. Remove the greens from the ice water and dry them well before placing on the baking sheet. Place the capers and rosemary on the baking sheet too.

Oven Preparation

Thirty minutes prior to baking, move the oven rack to the middle and preheat the oven to 450°F (230°C; gas mark 8), allowing time for the oven to come to full temperature.

Shaping

1. Moisten your hands with water or a bit of oil. If the dough did not come out of the bowl in a smooth ball, you will need to gently shape it into a ball shape with the smoothest side up.

2. Transfer the ball, smooth side up, to the oiled baking sheet. Begin dimpling and stretching evenly all around the ball to create a disc shape. The dough will most likely want to spring back, in which case just allow it to rest for 5 to 10 minutes, uncovered, on the parchment.

3. Continue to use your fingers and palms to gently coerce the dough into a disc shape about 10 inches (25 cm) in diameter and about 1 inch (2.5 cm) thick. Remember, as you decorate the dough will continue to rise and stretch out a bit so be sure to leave a little room around the edge of your baking sheet. Coat the dough with the remaining 2 tablespoons oil.

4. Divide the dark dough into 3 equal-size pieces on a lightly floured surface. Using your hands, roll out each piece into a thin rope, about 18 inches (46 cm) long, slightly tapering the ends for the roots. Braid or twist the 3 strands together (see page 27), leaving 4- to 5-inch-long (10 to 12.5 cm) unbraided ends. Cut 8 to 10 pieces off the long ends to be used to fill in roots and branches.

5. Lay the braided strands down the middle of the disc of dough. Spread the bottom strands out to create roots at the base, adding a few more pieces, then twisting the strands and pieces, as well as forming them into small loops for a root-like effect. Do the same at the top of the tree, spreading them out to create branches flowing in all directions across the top of the dough, also adding additional branches. Gently press the trunk, roots, and branches into the dough.

Decorating

1. Begin by placing a variety of colored flowers all over the tree branches.

2. Place a few scallion stems coming off the roots and place flowers on top of the stems. To set them in place use the back end of a chopstick to push the stems down into the dough deeply. Do this at the top and bottom of each stem as well as a few spots in between.

3. Decorate the branches and flowers with the scallion leaves.

4. Place the sage and basil leaves, rosemary needles, and capers in various spots as leaves around the branches and around the base of the tree as leaves that have fallen to the ground.

5. Once you have finished decorating, survey the surface and deflate any large air bubbles with a toothpick or skewer, leaving smaller ones intact (docking). Using piano-style finger motions, gently dimple the dough again. Ultimately, you want to see an uneven bubbly texture, about 1½ to 2 inches (4 to 5 cm) thick in various spots. If the focaccia is flat, allow it to rest for 8 to 10 minutes in a warm, draft-free place.

Baking

1. Just before placing your focaccia in the oven, check the decorations to be sure they are all snug. Secure any that look to be popping off, using the chopstick, a skewer, or your fingers.

2. Add finishing salt (if using) and place the focaccia on the middle rack of the oven.

3. Bake for 8 minutes at 450°F (230°C; gas mark 8). Reduce the heat to 375°F (190°C; gas mark 5) and check the decorations again. If any are popping off, coerce them back into the dough by gently and carefully poking down. You don't want to burn yourself. Bake for 10 to 16 more minutes, until the focaccia is golden brown and crisp on the edges.

4. Remove from the oven and let cool for at least 5 to 10 minutes before cutting.

Wood Grain Charcuterie Board

Can you have your charcuterie board and eat it too? Why, yes, you can! Serve your cheeses, meats, vegetables, fruits, and dips on this delicious edible board that is sure to be the talk of any get-together.

YIELD: 1 FOCACCIA

1 recipe for Basic White Focaccia (page 30) or Basic Whole Wheat Focaccia (page 34), with additional ingredients and instructions (see step 1 of Dough Preparation)

1 tablespoon dark cocoa powder

3 tablespoons plus 1 teaspoon extra-virgin olive or neutral oil, divided

1 tablespoon poppy seeds

1 tablespoon black sesame seeds

1 tablespoon brown flaxseeds

1 tablespoon everything bagel seasoning

Flour, for dusting

Finishing salt, to taste (optional)

Special Tools

Coffee grinder or mini chopper fitted with grinding blade

1 or 2 (4-ounce, or 120-ml) ramekins (3 inches, or 7.5 cm, in size)

Dough Preparation

1. Prepare the basic dough as directed in the recipe, adding an extra ¼ cup (37 g) bread flour, ¼ teaspoon kosher salt, and ¼ teaspoon oil when those ingredients are used. This should make a slightly firmer dough.

2. After mixing in the salt and oil, divide the dough in half and place in separate bowls.

3. Sprinkle the dark cocoa powder over one of the doughs and blend until incorporated, using a combination of stretching and folding, as well as kneading if necessary.

4. When the cocoa is evenly incorporated, allow both doughs to rest in separate bowls for 15 minutes, covered, in a warm, draft-free place.

5. Move onto the development and second rise as directed in the recipe.

Oven Preparation

Thirty minutes prior to baking, move the oven rack to the middle and preheat the oven to 450°F (230°C; gas mark 8), allowing time for the oven to come to full temperature.

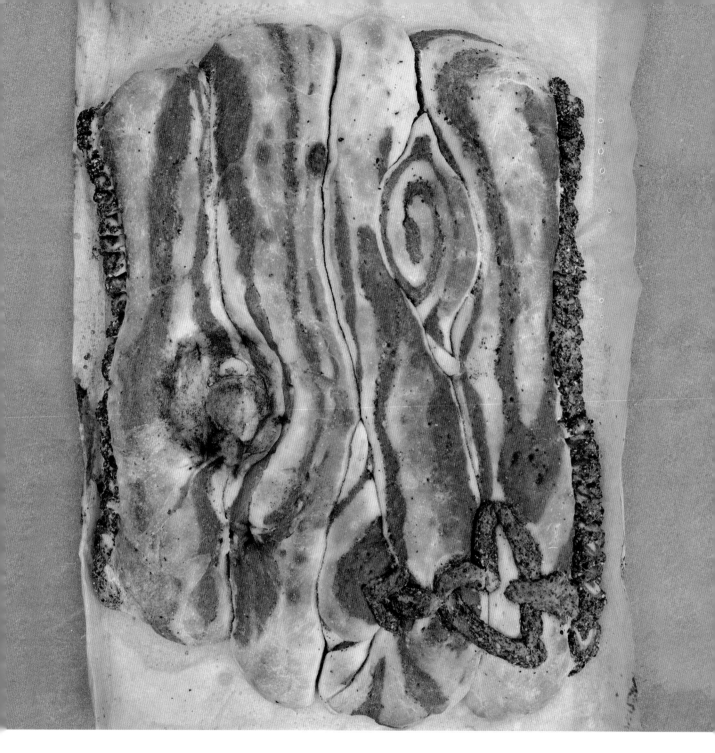

Seed Garnish Preparation

Add all the seeds and everything bagel seasoning to the coffee grinder or mini chopper. Pulse the seeds until a sandy texture. Do not overgrind.

Shaping and Decorating

1. Prepare a piece of parchment about the size of your intended focaccia and lay it on an 18 x 13-inch (46 x 33 cm) baking sheet. Coat the parchment with 1 tablespoon of the oil.

2. Cut off a golf ball–size piece of the darker dough and set aside. This will be the bark and heart shape.

3. On a lightly floured surface, use a rolling pin to roll out the uncolored dough on a lightly floured surface. Shape it into a 6 x 12-inch (15 x 30 cm) rectangle. Set aside. Repeat with the large piece of dark dough. Brush away any excess flour from the uncolored dough and spritz with water to moisten. Sprinkle the ground-seed mixture all over the dough, reserving 1 tablespoon. Lay the dark dough on top of the seeded dough, trying to match up all sides. Run a rolling pin over the top to set it in place.

4. With the dough positioned lengthwise on your work space, roll it upward into a tight log, starting from the bottom-left side. Once you have created a log, roll it back and forth to increase the length to about 15 inches (38 cm), then pinch the dough together at the seam. Use a paring knife or bench knife to cut two 1-inch-thick (2.5 cm) slices off either end. Set aside.

5. Lay the log, seam side down, on the work surface. Use a paring knife to slice lengthwise down the middle of the log, creating 2 sides. Cut each side in half lengthwise so that you have 4 pieces.

6. With the oiled baking sheet next to your work area, begin with the first strip by carefully transferring it to the sheet and laying it lengthwise, wood grain side up, 1½ inches (4 cm) from the side of the baking sheet. Next, place one of the reserved discs with the most prominent rings facing up on the work surface and, using your fingers, pinch the opposite ends, pulling slightly to elongate the disc and create points about 1 inch (2.5 cm) long on either side. Lay the elongated disc against the first layer, approximately 1 inch (2.5 cm) from the top or bottom of the dough. Neatly tuck in this shape lengthwise against the first dough strip as the first "knot" in your board. If the dough is dry, lightly spritz it with water, which will help the strips stay together. Take the next dough strip and lay it so that it is slightly misaligned with the first strip to give a natural look of imperfect wood. Be sure the layers are snug up against each other. The "knot" will cause a slight bulge, which is perfectly fine. With the remaining reserved disc, shape it as you did the first disc, then lay it on the opposite end from the other knot at the left of the second strip. Lay the third dough strip, wood grain side up, against the second strip and slightly misaligned. Tuck the second and third strips snug around the knot. Lay down the last dough strip, wood grain side up and slightly misaligned. Gently adjust as needed to be sure all edges are touching and tucked together. You can pinch the layers together where they meet along each layer; however, it is okay to have the ends slightly separated to give an authentic look to the wood board. With the palm of a wet hand, gently pat the entire surface of the dough down allowing the layers to level out a bit.

7. Sprinkle the reserved ground-seed mixture on your work surface. Begin rolling out the reserved piece of dark dough into a log shape, using both hands in a back-and-forth motion, in the seed mixture. This will create a bark-like texture and appearance.

Try to use up all the seeds and roll the dough to about 24 inches (60 cm) long and no more than ½ inch (1 cm) thick. Cut a 2-inch (5 cm) piece off an end of the rope and set aside. Cut the larger piece in half horizontally. Roll the two halves of the seeded rope one more time with your palms to ensure the seeds blend into the dough.

8. Spritz the long sides of the dough board with water, then place each piece of seeded dough along the sides, tucking them in tightly to the dough. Use a small pair of kitchen scissors to make small snips, moving down the seeded dough edges, to give the effect of rough bark.

9. Roll out the reserved piece of seeded dough into a thin, long rope. Shape it into a heart and place it wherever you like on the dough board.

10. Coat the dough with 2 tablespoons of the oil, then dimple it. Be sure the focaccia does not have any large air bubbles—these should be docked with a toothpick or skewer. If the dough layers appear to be separating, spritz them with a little water and carefully adjust by lifting or pushing the sides back together. If the pieces bunch up, pat them down with the palm of your hand.

11. Cut a small piece(s) of parchment to fit under the ramekin(s)—you can use one or two ramekins depending on how many dips you would like to place on the baked board. Oil the parchment on both sides with the remaining 1 teaspoon oil and lay it on the focaccia in the preferred spot(s). Place the ramekin(s) on the oiled parchment and gently push into the dough, just enough to make an indentation, about ½ inch (1 cm). Leave at least 1-inch (2.5 cm) space around the ramekin(s).

12. With the palm of your hands, press down around the dough to ensure an even surface. If any air bubbles form, deflate with a toothpick or skewer. Cover and let rise in a warm, draft free place for 10 to 15 minutes. Ultimately, you want to see an uneven bubbly texture, about 1½ to 2 inches (4 to 5 cm) thick in various spots. If the focaccia is flat, allow it to rest for 8 to 10 minutes in a warm, draft-free place.

Baking

1. Add finishing salt (if using) and place the focaccia on the middle rack of the oven.

2. Bake for 10 minutes at 450°F (230°C; gas mark 8). Reduce the heat to 375°F (190°C; gas mark 5) and carefully remove the ramekins and parchment paper with an oven mitt. Be very careful as the ramekins will be hot. Bake for another 10 to 16 minutes, until the focaccia is golden brown and crisp on the edges.

3. Remove from the oven and let cool for at least 5 to 10 minutes.

4. Fill the well(s) in the bread with your favorite dip(s). Lay out various charcuterie veggies, meats, and pickled items on top of the "board."

Sandcastle

There is some refrigeration involved with this project, but it can happen during the final rise or even overnight. Cold dough is essential to this recipe for shaping. Bake away the winter doldrums with this fun and delicious sandcastle that's a perfect indoor activity for kids as well. This dough is shaped to be a pull-apart bread brushed with a molasses vinaigrette for a deep pretzel-like flavor.

YIELD: 1 FOCACCIA

1 recipe for Basic White Focaccia (page 30) or Basic Whole Wheat Focaccia (page 34), with additional ingredients and instructions (see step 1 of Dough Preparation)

1 tablespoon extra-virgin olive or neutral oil

1 teaspoon lemon juice

Bowl of ice water

1 small bunch chives or 2 scallions

1 large red carrot, peeled

1 large orange carrot, peeled

1 red mini sweet pepper

1 yellow mini sweet pepper

1 orange mini sweet pepper

1 small green bell pepper

1 small red onion

6 to 10 pitted black olives

1 shallot

3 mini potatoes (a mix of blue or purple and white)

2 tablespoons white sesame seeds or golden flaxseeds

1 teaspoon black sesame seeds

1 teaspoon poppy seeds

Molasses Vinaigrette (see Note on page 123) or extra-virgin olive, for brushing

Pretzel or finishing salt, to taste (optional)

Dough Preparation

1. Prepare the basic dough as directed in the recipe, adding an extra ¼ cup (37 g) bread flour and ¼ teaspoon kosher salt when those ingredients are added to make a slightly firmer dough.

2. After 1 hour of room-temperature development and rise, shape the dough into a ball, lightly oil, and place, covered, in the refrigerator for the last hour of rise. The dough will roll out easier when cold.

Vegetable Preparation

1. Prepare two pieces of parchment about the size of your intended focaccia and lay them on two 18 x 13-inch (46 x 33 cm) baking sheets. Coat the parchment on one of the baking sheets with the oil.

2. Add the lemon juice to the bowl of ice water to keep the greens bright. Place the chives or scallions in the ice water.

3. From the wider ends of the carrots, make six or seven ¼-inch-wide (6 mm) slices lengthwise, 3 inches (7.5 cm) long, for panels for the castle doors. Round their tops with a paring knife. From the remaining parts of the carrots, use a julienne peeler to slice 9 to 12 strips for the flag poles and to outline the turrets.

4. Cut a pennant or flag shape from each of the peppers so that you have a variety of colors. Also cut 1 pennant or flag shape out of the purple part of the red onion.

5. Pat the olives dry. Slice them in half lengthwise for windows.

6. Slice the shallot into ¼-inch-thick (6 mm) slices to be used for seashells.

7. Thinly slice the potatoes in half lengthwise, then in half again, for the castle steps.

8. Remove the chives or scallions from the lemon water and pat dry. Trim the chives to 2 to 3 inches (5 to 7.5 cm) in length to be used for seaweed or grass. If using scallions, slice them in half lengthwise, then align the pieces on a cutting board and cut each half into 3 slices lengthwise.

9. Move all the vegetables to the unoiled baking sheet, keeping things separate and organized by color and sizes for ease of use during the decorating process. Place the seeds on the baking sheet too.

Oven Preparation

Thirty minutes prior to baking, move the oven rack to the middle and preheat the oven to 450°F (230°C; gas mark 8), allowing time for the oven to come to full temperature.

Shaping

1. Remove the dough from the refrigerator and place it on a lightly floured work surface. Use a rolling pin to roll it out to a 16 x 11-inch (40 x 28 cm) rectangle. Transfer the rolled-out dough to the oiled baking sheet, laying the focaccia vertically in front of you. Brush the dough with the molasses vinaigrette.

2. Use a pizza cutter or knife to cut off the top corners about 3 inches (7.5 cm) down from each of the longest sides. Cut each triangle in half, then cut only 1 triangle in half again, into 2 smaller triangles, for a total of 5 triangles. Set aside. Use the pizza cutter or knife again to cut the main piece of dough into 1-inch (2.5 cm) strips lengthwise, creating slice marks but not cutting all the way through the dough. This is the castle base, and the cuts will result in a puffy, layering effect that will be easy to pull apart.

3. Place the largest triangle as the top piece and smaller ones, descending in size, down the sides of the dough. Be sure the triangles overlap each other slightly.

Decorating

1. Be sure to gently press the decorations into the dough. Use more molasses vinaigrette, if needed, to help decorations adhere.

2. Starting from the bottom edge of the focaccia, place 3 rows of potato slices in alternating colors for the castle steps—one row in the center and one on either side. (If desired, you can brush the potatoes with melted butter or olive oil for an extra crispy texture.)

3. Use 4 or 5 thick carrot slices grouped together and overlapping, with the rounded ends at the top, to make a door shape above the central steps. Place a single carrot slice above the outer rows of steps for smaller doors.

4. Place the chives or scallion strips in between the steps as seaweed or beach grass, fanning the strips out slightly. Place the shallot seashells around the chives or scallions.

5. Place the black olive halves right below the triangular sections of dough for windows for the turrets.

6. Use the julienned carrot strips as poles for the pepper and onion flags and place the flags on each triangular section. Also outline the turrets with the carrot strips.

7. Scatter the sesame and poppy seeds all over the dough for a sand effect.

8. Once you have finished decorating, survey the surface and deflate any large air bubbles with a toothpick or skewer, leaving smaller ones intact (docking). Using piano-style finger motions, gently dimple the dough. Ultimately, you want to see an uneven bubbly texture, about 1½ to 2 inches (4 to 5 cm) thick in various spots. If the focaccia is flat, allow it to rest for 8 to 10 minutes in a warm, draft-free place.

Baking

1. Just before placing your focaccia in the oven, check the decorations to be sure they are all snug. Secure any that look to be popping off, using a chopstick, skewer, or your fingers.

2. Add the pretzel or finishing salt (if using) and place the focaccia on the middle rack of the oven.

3. Bake for 8 minutes at 450°F (230°C; gas mark 8). Reduce the heat to 375°F (190°C; gas mark 5) and check the decorations again. If any are popping off, coerce them back into the dough by gently and carefully poking down. You don't want to burn yourself. Bake for 10 to 16 more minutes, until the focaccia is golden brown and crisp on the edges.

4. Remove from the oven and let cool for at least 5 to 10 minutes before cutting.

> **NOTE**
> To make Molasses Vinaigrette, blend together 2 tablespoons of molasses or olive oil with 1 teaspoon of apple cider vinegar and 1 teaspoon of water.

Happy Trail Mix

Seed and nut trails, trees, rocks, and mountains, along with an apricot sunset, blend together in this delicious Bob Ross–style sweet focaccia. The natural colors of the seeds are perfect for this inviting landscape. And remember: There are no mistakes, just happy accidents.

YIELD: 1 FOCACCIA

1 recipe for Sweet Focaccia (page 41)

1 tablespoon neutral oil

1 tablespoon golden flaxseeds

1 tablespoon brown flaxseeds

1 tablespoon black sesame seeds

1 tablespoon white sesame seeds

1 tablespoon English pumpkin seeds

1 tablespoon pumpkin seeds

1 tablespoon millet seeds

1 tablespoon poppy or chia seeds

1 tablespoon sunflower seeds

3 tablespoons chopped pistachios

Almond slices (optional)

1 dried apricot

½ cup (150 g) Chocolate Hazelnut Filling (page 166 or store-bought) or ½ cup Cinnamon Filling (page 167)

Flour, for dusting

Honey glue (2 tablespoons honey mixed with 2 tablespoons water), for brushing

Egg wash (1 egg beaten with ¼ cup, or 60 ml, water) or whole milk, for brushing (optional)

Special Tools

2-ounce (60 ml) paper cups (see Notes on page 127), for holding seeds and nuts

9 x 13-inch (23 x 33 cm) baking dish or 8 x 11-inch (20 x 28 cm) Pyrex dish

Food-safe paint brushes (used only for food) in various sizes, including a medium-size brush for brushing off excess seeds and nuts

Dough Preparation

1. Prepare the dough according to the recipe instructions to its second rise, placing the dough in the refrigerator for the last 30 minutes of the second rise. (This will make rolling out the dough easier.)

2. Coat the baking dish with the oil or line with oiled parchment paper. Set aside.

Topping Preparation

1. Gather all the toppings you desire to use in your art project and separate the seeds into separate small cups or bowls.

2. Soak the dried apricot in water for 5 minutes, then pat dry.

Oven Preparation

Thirty minutes prior to baking, move the oven rack to the middle and preheat the oven to 350°F (180°C; gas mark 4), allowing time for the oven to come to full temperature.

Shaping and Filling

1. Place the chilled dough on a lightly floured work surface. Use a rolling pin to roll it out to a 21 x 7-inch (53 x 18 cm) rectangle. This dough should be fairly easy to roll out due to the enriched ingredients and not spring back too much.

2. Use a spatula to spread the chocolate hazelnut or cinnamon filling evenly across two-thirds of the dough, leaving ½ inch (1 cm) uncoated around all the edges to prevent leakage.

3. Fold the dough rectangle into thirds as if you were folding a letter to go in an envelope. Starting from the side that is not covered with filling, fold inward over the

filling by about 7 inches (18 cm). Next, take the other side that is covered with filling and carefully fold over the uncovered layer. You now have a trifold dough full of chocolate hazelnut or cinnamon filling.

4. Use the rolling pin to gently give one or two rolls across the folded dough to secure. Stop rolling if it appears that any filling is squeezing out and pinch that end closed.

5. Cut a piece of parchment paper that is 3 inches (7.5 cm) larger than the dough on all sides and coat it with the remaining 2 teaspoons oil. Move the dough to the oiled parchment and dock it (page 17). It is very important to poke a toothpick or skewer throughout the dough at this point and deflate any bubbles that have formed in the dough. It also prevents trapped air from puffing up and creating an uneven bake in the oven.

Decorating

1. This can get a bit messy, so it's a good idea to work over newspaper to help make the cleanup easy.

2. Lift the dough using the overhang of the parchment onto a wire rack or elevated surface over the newspaper. Dust the dough with flour. You now have about 1 hour before baking to decorate the dough. It is helpful to already have an idea about the design that you have sketched or printed out so that you can move through this project swiftly before the dough rises too much. If that happens, place the dough in the freezer for 10 to 15 minutes to slow the rise.

3. Position the dough landscape. Use a paint brush to paint the honey glue on the dough, working on one area at a time. Begin at the bottom and work your way out if you are doing a linear design. If you are working on a floral or circular design, work from the center out.

4. Sprinkle the desired seeds, nuts, or dried fruit carefully over the honey painted areas. Use a clean paint brush to carefully brush away any loose particles. Alternate colors to give depth and dimension to your design.

5. Make a frame around the edges of the scene with the almond slices (if using) and honey glue.

6. Using the parchment overhang, carefully lift the decorated dough and place it in the prepared baking dish. Trim off the overhanging parchment. Dock the dough again with a toothpick or skewer to poke holes throughout the dough to ensure an even rise on the bake.

7. After decorating, allow the dough to rest in a warm, draft-free place, lightly covered, for 15 to 20 minutes before baking. The dough should double to about 2 inches (5 cm) thick.

Baking

1. Just before placing your sweet dough in the oven, check the decorations to be sure they are all snug. Secure any that look to be popping off, using a chopstick, skewer, or your fingers.

2. Brush the dough areas with egg wash (if using) to create shine.

3. Place the focaccia on the middle rack and bake for 25 to 28 minutes, until golden brown, checking the decorations after 8 minutes of baking time. If any decorations are popping off, carefully place them back on and return to oven for the rest of the baking time.

4. Remove from the oven and let cool completely before cutting. Any leftovers should be stored in the refrigerator.

NOTES

- I recommend using paper cups to hold the seeds and nuts because you can pinch the tops of them to control the amount that comes out when sprinkling on your dough.

- You can also use stencils (page 27) or cookie cutters to add shapes to your design. Carefully brush the honey glue inside the stencil or cookie cutter shapes and lightly sprinkle the seeds or nuts into the shape. Carefully lift the stencil or cutter and brush away any excess seeds or nuts.

Solar System

A round focaccia with all the planets circling the sun—perfect for a solstice party. Or align the planets to coordinate with a day of birth for a new spin on a birthday cake. If you do a quick google search of "planet placement for month/day/year," it will offer you images of both the heliocentric view (sun in the center) and geocentric view (Earth in the center) of their birth date. How fun is that?

YIELD: 1 FOCACCIA

1 recipe for Basic Whole Wheat Focaccia (page 34) or Dark Multigrain Focaccia (page 38)

3 tablespoons extra-virgin olive or neutral oil, divided

1 small red bell pepper

1 small orange bell pepper

1 small green bell pepper

1 small red onion

1 small zucchini

1 large white carrot, peeled

1 mini purple potato

1 small leek

1 large yellow beet, peeled, or yellow bell pepper

1 fresh fig

1 tablespoon poppy seeds

1 tablespoon black sesame or nigella seeds

Finishing salt, to taste (optional)

Special Tools

Circle cookie cutters in various sizes

Mini and small star-shaped cookie cutters

Mini diamond- and leaf-shaped cookie cutters

Dough Preparation
Prepare the dough according to the recipe instructions to its second rise.

Vegetable Preparation

1. Prepare two pieces of parchment about the size of your intended focaccia and lay them on two 18 x 13-inch (46 x 33 cm) baking sheets. Coat the parchment on one of the sheets with 1 tablespoon of the oil.

2. Begin by cutting a variety of circle sizes from the bell peppers and red onion. Cut a 2-inch (5 cm) round from the zucchini that is ¼ inch (6 mm) thick for a small green planet.

3. Slice the white carrot into eight ¼-inch-thick (6 mm) rounds, then cut out 4 each of mini and small stars with the cookie cutters. Use a paring knife to cut star tails from the red onion. Cut a 2-inch (5 cm) strip from the red onion for Saturn's ring.

4. Cut out shapes from the flesh of the zucchini slice with the diamond- and leaf-shaped

cookie cutters. Fill those spaces with the same shapes cut from the green pepper and purple potato.

5. Slice a 1-inch-wide (2.5 cm) leek round that is ¼ inch (6 mm) thick. Cut a ring from the red onion that will fit around the leek.

6. Use a julienne peeler to cut the remaining white carrot into 4 or 5 slices, then cut the slices into small bits for cosmic dust.

7. Cut a nice slice for the sun from the yellow beet. You can also cut a large circle from an orange or yellow bell pepper. Cut a ½-inch-thick (1 cm) horizontal slice from the fig for a planet.

8. Move all the vegetables to the unoiled baking sheet, keeping things separate and organized by color and sizes for ease of use during the decorating process. Place the seeds on the baking sheet too.

Oven Preparation

Thirty minutes prior to baking, move the oven rack to the middle and preheat the oven to 450°F (230°C; gas mark 8), allowing time for the oven to come to full temperature.

Shaping

1. To create the universe onto which your planets and stars will rest, moisten your hands with water or a bit of oil. If the dough did not come out of the bowl in a smooth ball, you will need to gently shape it into a ball shape with the smoothest side up.

2. Transfer the ball, smooth side up, to the oiled baking sheet. Begin dimpling and stretching evenly all around the ball to create a disc shape. The dough will most likely want to spring back, in which case just allow it to rest for 5 to 10 minutes, uncovered, on the parchment.

3. Continue to use your fingers and palms to gently coerce the dough into a disc shape about 10 inches (25 cm) in diameter and about 1 inch (2.5 cm) thick. Remember, as you decorate the dough will continue to rise and stretch out a bit so be sure to leave a little room around the edge of your baking sheet.

4. Coat the dough with the remaining 2 tablespoons oil.

Decorating

1. Start with the centerpiece by placing the beet or pepper circle in the center for the sun and place the smaller circles around the sun across the dough for the planets. Place the red strip of onion on a yellow planet for Saturn's ring.

2. Lay the stars in random places and place onion tails behind them.

3. Place the zucchini slice on the dough and fill the center with different colored vegetable pieces.

4. Place the leek round with the red onion ring around it.

5. Mix the seeds together, then sprinkle them all over the dough, along with the small bits of white carrot.

6. Once you have finished decorating, survey the surface and deflate any large air bubbles with a toothpick or skewer, leaving smaller ones intact (docking). Using piano-style finger motions, gently dimple the dough again. Ultimately, you want to see an uneven bubbly texture, about 1½ to 2 inches (4 to 5 cm) thick in various spots. If the focaccia is flat, allow it to rest for 8 to 10 minutes in a warm, draft-free place.

Baking

1. Just before placing your focaccia in the oven, check the decorations to be sure they are all snug. Secure any that look to be popping off, using a chopstick, skewer, or your fingers.

2. Add finishing salt (if using) and place the focaccia on the middle rack of the oven.

3. Bake for 8 minutes, then reduce the heat to 375°F (190°C; gas mark 5) and check the decorations again. If any are popping off, coerce them back into the dough by gently and carefully poking down. You don't want to burn yourself. Bake for 10 to 16 more minutes, until the focaccia is golden brown and crisp on the edges.

4. Remove from the oven and let cool for at least 5 to 10 minutes before cutting.

Pomegranate

This focaccia brings to mind the classic debate if a tomato is a fruit or a vegetable. But what about a pomegranate focaccia made with vegetables?

YIELD: 1 FOCACCIA

1 recipe for Basic White Focaccia (page 30) or Basic Whole Wheat Focaccia (page 34)

3 tablespoons extra-virgin olive or neutral oil, divided

5 red mini sweet peppers

5 yellow mini sweet peppers

5 orange mini sweet peppers

1 small red onion

6 pitted kalamata olives

Dough Preparation

Prepare the dough according to the recipe instructions to its second rise.

Vegetable Preparation

1. Prepare two pieces of parchment about the size of your intended focaccia and lay them on two 18 x 13-inch (46 x 33 cm) baking sheets. Coat the parchment on one of the sheets with 1 tablespoon of the oil.

2. Trim the tops of the mini peppers. Slice the peppers in half lengthwise and remove the seeds and pith. Cut the halves lengthwise into ⅛-inch-thick (3 mm) slices.

3. Remove and discard the outer layer of the red onion. Cut the onion into slices about the same thickness as the peppers. Separate the darker purple slices from the lighter slices.

4. Pat the kalamata olives dry, then mince them.

5. Move all the vegetables to the unoiled baking sheet, keeping things separate and organized by color and sizes for ease of use during the decorating process.

Oven Preparation

Thirty minutes prior to baking, move the oven rack to the middle and preheat the oven to 450°F (230°C; gas mark 8), allowing time for the oven to come to full temperature.

Shaping

1. Moisten your hands with water or a bit of oil. If the dough did not come out of the bowl in a smooth ball, you will need to gently shape it into a ball shape with the smoothest side up. Transfer the ball, smooth side up, to the oiled baking sheet. Begin dimpling and stretching evenly all around the ball to create a circle with a handle-like

piece of dough pulled out at the top. Make four 1-inch (2.5 cm) cuts in the top and pull each piece to a point to shape. Bend these slightly to give a burst-like effect at the top of the circular dough. The dough will most likely want to spring back, in which case just allow it to rest for 5 to 10 minutes, uncovered, on the parchment.

2. Continue to use your fingers and palms to gently coerce the dough into a circle about 10 inches (25 cm) in diameter and about 1 inch (2.5 cm) thick. Remember, as you decorate the dough will continue to rise and stretch out a bit so be sure to leave a little room around the edge of your baking sheet.

3. Coat the dough with the remaining 2 tablespoons oil.

Decorating

1. Place the minced kalamata olives on the top center, just below the four-pointed piece of dough.

2. Beginning at the base of the circle, place darker red pepper slices on the dough, working up the sides of the circle. Let the natural curve of the sliced peppers follow the curve of the shaped dough. Surround the olives with more red pepper slices. It is important to crowd them in as the dough will rise and puff in the oven.

3. Place the orange pepper slices, some intertwining with the red slices and filling in around the bottom and sides. Fill in the center of the focaccia with the yellow pepper slices. Cover the tips of the fruit with yellow pepper slices blending into red slices at the base.

4. Place the red onion slices around the top section. The natural curve of the onion should follow the shape of the dough. Interlace some red pepper slices with the purple onions for a darker shading effect.

5. Once you have finished decorating, survey the surface and deflate any large air bubbles with a toothpick or skewer, leaving smaller ones intact (docking). Using piano-style finger motions, gently dimple the dough again. Ultimately, you want to see an uneven bubbly texture, about 1½ to 2 inches (4 to 5 cm) thick in various spots. If the focaccia is flat, allow it to rest for 8 to 10 minutes in a warm, draft-free place.

Baking

1. Just before placing your focaccia in the oven, check the decorations to be sure they are all snug. Secure any that look to be popping off, using a chopstick or your fingers.

2. Add finishing salt (if using) and place the focaccia on the middle rack of the oven.

3. Bake for 8 minutes at 450°F (230°C; gas mark 8). Reduce the heat to 375°F (190°C; gas mark 5) and check the decorations again. If any are popping off, coerce them back into the dough by gently and carefully poking down. You don't want to burn yourself. Bake for 10 to 16 more minutes, until the focaccia is golden brown and crisp on the edges.

4. Remove from the oven and let cool for at least 5 to 10 minutes before cutting.

Holidays & Special Occasions

Who doesn't love to gather and celebrate with family and friends around the holidays or even a major sporting event? These focaccia projects are just a few ways to express creativity around a special occasion or to encourage you to bring a beautiful, unique, and memorable food to start a new tradition.

Valentine's Day Roses

This focaccia is perfect for Valentine's Day, but it doesn't have to be a special occasion to give your sweetheart "red roses." Any candlelight dinner is made more special with a focaccia full of roses—a savory way to say I love you.

YIELD: 1 FOCACCIA

1 recipe for Basic White Focaccia (page 30) or Basic Whole Wheat Focaccia (page 34)

4 tablespoons extra-virgin olive or neutral oil, divided

1 teaspoon lemon juice

Bowl of ice water

12 to 15 leaves arugula

6 sprigs lacy herb (such as dill or fennel)

4 scallions

2 large whole roasted red peppers (see page 25 for how to roast your own)

1 to 2 mini sweet peppers (your choice of color)

8 to 10 pitted black or kalamata olives

2 tablespoons crumbled feta or goat cheese

Flour, for dusting

Dark cocoa powder, for stenciling (optional)

Honey glue (equal parts honey and water), for sticking if needed

Finishing salt, to taste (optional)

Special Tools

Mini flower-shaped (or shape of your choice) cookie cutters

Stenciling pattern (optional)

Dough Preparation

Prepare the dough according to the recipe instructions to its second rise.

Vegetable Preparation

1. Prepare two pieces of parchment about the size of your intended focaccia and lay them on two 18 x 13-inch (46 x 33 cm) baking sheets. Coat the parchment on one of the sheets with 1 tablespoon of the oil.

2. Add the lemon juice to the bowl of ice water to keep the greens bright. Place the arugula and lacy herbs in the ice water.

3. For the stems, cut off ½ inch (1 cm) from the bottom of each scallion, and then vertically slice down each scallion on the bias into 4 pieces. Place in the ice water.

4. Cut the roasted red peppers into ½-inch-wide (1 cm) strips down the long side of each pepper. Make around 18 to 24 strips.

5. Trim the tops of the mini peppers. Cut the peppers in half lengthwise and remove the seeds and pith, then cut each pepper half lengthwise. Flatten the halves and

cut out 10 flowers with the cookie cutters. These can be any color you like, as they will be used for decorating the paper wrapping.

6. Pat the olives dry. Cut them in half crosswise.

7. Move all the vegetables to the unoiled baking sheet, keeping things separate and organized by color and sizes for ease of use during the decorating process. Remove the greens from the ice water and dry them well before placing on the baking sheet. Place the crumbled cheese on the baking sheet too.

Oven Preparation

Thirty minutes prior to baking, move the oven rack to the middle and preheat the oven to 450°F (230°C; gas mark 8), allowing time for the oven to come to full temperature.

Shaping

1. Gently flip the dough onto the oiled baking sheet. It should look like a round dome. Cut two 1 x 3-inch (2.5 x 7.5 cm) pieces from either side of the bottom of the dome, leaving a slightly pointed bottom. Combine these pieces into a ball and set aside; it will be used as part of the paper wrapping of the bouquet.

2. Shape the remaining dough into a heart shape. First make a cut 3 inches (7.5 cm) deep in the center at the top. Gently pull down the bottom part of the dough at the center, aligned with the top cut, to create a point. Try not to rip the dough as you work. Coat the top of dough with the remaining 2 tablespoons oil. Using fingers that are arched and separated, begin to stretch the dough gently, creating 2 rounded arches as you spread the dough while dimpling it (page 17). If the dough becomes resistant to stretching, let it rest for 5 to 8 minutes, then continue to shape it.

3. Place the reserved dough ball on a lightly floured surface and use a rolling pin to roll it out into a flat rectangle, about 4 x 6 inches (10 x 15 cm). Dust with flour as needed.

Decorating

1. Starting with the scallion stems, place them on the heart-shaped dough, gathering them at the bottom right of the heart and spreading them out across the top to fill the space. The bottoms of the stems will be gathered in what looks like paper wrapping with the reserved rectangle of dough. As you place each stem, "lock" it in place by pushing it down into the dough with a chopstick. To set them in place use the back end of the chopstick to push the stems down into the dough deeply, at the top and bottom and a few spots in between.

2. Place the lacy herbs in a few places toward the top and outer edges in among the stems. These will be baby's breath in between the roses. Use tweezers, the chopstick, or a skewer to help spread out the wispy herb. Adorn the fine leaves with the feta or goat cheese crumbles.

3. Place the arugula leaves around the scallion stems, overlapping in some places. Be sure to leave room for the roses as you work.

4. Make a small notch in your dough to hold each rose. Using kitchen scissors, snip a ½-inch (1 cm) X shape in the spots where you will be positioning the roses. Do not cut through the dough, but cut just deep enough to make a small opening to snugly place the roses.

5. Pat the red pepper strips dry. Wrap one around your finger, with the inside portion of the pepper facing outward. Carefully move it off your finger and place the curled-up pepper in position. Secure it by gently pressing it into the small notch you just made. Continue wrapping and placing more roses across your design, filling the space. Bend the edges of each rose so that they curl over slightly to resemble petals.

6. Place the olive halves, narrow ends up, in the center of each rose, making sure they are tucked into the pepper.

7. Before placing the reserved rectangle of dough for the paper wrapping on your design, stencil a pattern onto it using cocoa powder (follow the directions on page 27 for stenciling).

8. Place the dough, stenciled or not, over the base of the stems, creating folds and wrinkles in the surface, and pulling up to one side to create a wrapped paper–like texture. Adorn the paper with the mini flower shapes and a few loosely placed cheese crumbles. If needed, use a little honey glue to help the little pieces adhere to the stenciled dough.

9. Once you have finished decorating, survey the surface and deflate any large air bubbles with a toothpick or skewer, leaving smaller ones intact (docking). Using piano-style finger motions, gently dimple the dough again. Ultimately, you want to see an uneven bubbly texture, about 1½ to 2 inches (4 to 5 cm) thick in various spots. If the focaccia is flat, allow it to rest for 8 to 10 minutes in a warm, draft-free place.

Baking

1. Just before placing your focaccia in the oven, check the decorations to be sure they are all snug. Secure any that look to be popping off, using the chopstick, a skewer, or your fingers.

2. Add finishing salt (if using) and place the focaccia on the middle rack of the oven.

3. Bake for 8 minutes at 450°F (230°C; gas mark 8). Reduce the heat to 375°F (190°C; gas mark 5) and check the decorations again. If any are popping off, coerce them back into the dough by gently and carefully poking down. You don't want to burn yourself. Bake for 10 to 16 more minutes, until the focaccia is golden brown and crisp on the edges.

4. Remove from the oven and let cool for at least 5 to 10 minutes before cutting.

Saint Patrick's Day Lucky Clover

Green is the theme of Saint Patrick's Day, and this bread is no exception. I like to use the dark multigrain focaccia for this clover-shaped bread, which is thick and hearty enough for slicing horizontally for sandwiches or enjoying as a pull-apart bread for dinner.

YIELD: 1 FOCACCIA

1 recipe for Dark Multigrain Focaccia (page 38) or Basic Whole Wheat Focaccia (page 34) with leek and sage flavor variation (page 33; optional)

3 tablespoons extra-virgin olive or neutral oil, divided

1 teaspoon lemon juice

Bowl of ice water

3 sprigs flat-leaf parsley

4 leaves arugula

4 scallions

1 large green bell pepper

1/3 cup (45 g) green hulled pumpkin seeds

Flour, for dusting

2 teaspoons ground black pepper and poppy seeds, for sprinkling (optional)

Special Tools

Medium heart-shaped cookie cutter (optional)

Dough Preparation

Prepare the dough according to the recipe instructions to its second rise.

Vegetable Preparation

1. Prepare two pieces of parchment about the size of your intended focaccia and lay them on two 18 x 13-inch (46 x 33 cm) baking sheets. Coat one of the parchment-lined baking sheets with 1 tablespoon of the oil.

2. Add the lemon juice to the bowl of ice water to keep the greens bright. Place the parsley and arugula in the ice water.

3. Trim the bottom and top of the scallions, about 1 inch (2.5 cm) from each end. Run a knife through the scallion lengthwise (on the bias). Do this twice to make a spray. Place the scallions in the ice water to encourage curling.

4. Trim the top of the green bell pepper and remove the seeds and pith. There are two cuts that can be made: Either cut out 4 heart shapes using the cookie cutter or cut the pepper into four ½-inch-wide (1 cm) slices horizontally to reveal beautiful, natural clover-shape rings. Both are pretty options.

5. Move all the vegetables to the unoiled baking sheet, keeping things separate and organized by color and sizes for ease of use during the decorating process. Remove the greens from the ice water and dry them well before placing on the baking sheet. Place the pumpkin seeds on the baking sheet too.

Oven Preparation

Thirty minutes prior to baking, move the oven rack to the middle and preheat the oven to 425°F (220°C; gas mark 7), allowing time for the oven to come to full temperature.

Shaping

1. Lightly dust a work surface with flour. Place the dough on the work surface and flatten it into a round disc. Use a bowl scraper to divide it into 4 equal-size pieces.

2. Using your hands, flatten each piece of dough into a 5 x 2-inch (12.5 x 5 cm) oblong shape.

3. Make a 1-inch (2.5 cm) cut in the center at the wider end of each dough piece and shape into a heart.

4. Move the dough hearts onto the oiled baking sheet with the pointed ends all facing into the center to create a clover shape. Gently push them together so they sit as one piece of dough.

5. Use a bowl scraper to make a divot from the center of each heart, going down to the point, to give the clover depth. Don't cut through the dough.

6. Coat the dough with the remaining 2 tablespoons oil.

Decorating

1. Place a green pepper heart on the bottom point of each heart shape.

2. Lay a scallion on each heart, starting from the top of the green pepper heart and spraying up and out to create a curve around each side of the dough hearts. You can add more curls to fill up empty space if you like. As you place each scallion, "lock" it in place by pushing it down into the dough with a chopstick. To set them in place, use the back end of the chopstick to push the scallions down into the dough deeply, at the top and bottom and a few spots in between.

3. Place the pumpkin seeds all around the edges of the dough to outline the clover shape.

4. Place the arugula leaves along the edges of the hearts to meet up with the pumpkin-seed outline.

5. Lastly, add the parsley leaves, pulled off in smaller sprigs of groups of three, inside the curves of the scallions.

6. Once you have finished decorating, place in a warm, draft-free place, lightly covered with a tea towel, for 15 minutes. Ultimately, you want to see an uneven bubbly texture, about 1½ to 2 inches (4 to 5 cm) thick in various spots. If the focaccia is flat, allow it to rest for a bit longer in a warm, draft-free place.

Baking

1. Just before placing your focaccia in the oven, check the decorations to be sure they are all snug. Secure any that look to be popping off, using the chopstick, a skewer, or your fingers.

2. Add the black pepper and poppy seeds (if using) and place the focaccia on the middle rack of the oven.

3. Immediately reduce the heat to 375°F (190°C; gas mark 5) and bake for 20 to 25 minutes, until the crust is deep brown.

4. Remove from the oven and let cool completely before cutting or pulling apart.

Easter Basket

The little chicks peeking out among the eggs and flowers make this focaccia adorable. The savory flavors will add a perfect balance to an Easter buffet.

YIELD: 1 FOCACCIA

1 recipe for Basic White Focaccia (page 30) or Basic Whole Wheat Focaccia (page 34)

2 teaspoons dark cocoa powder

3 tablespoons extra-virgin olive or neutral oil, divided

1 medium yellow squash

1 medium orange carrot, peeled

6 black peppercorns

2 red mini sweet peppers

2 yellow mini sweet peppers

2 orange mini sweet peppers

1 small red onion

1 small leek

1 large purple carrot, peeled

1 mini purple potato

Flour, for dusting

Finishing salt, to taste (optional)

Special Tools

2 inch (5 cm) circle cookie cutter

1 inch (2.5 cm) egg-shaped or oval cookie cutter

½ inch (1 cm) flower-shaped cookie cutter

Lattice cutter (optional)

Dough Preparation

1. Prepare the dough according to the recipe instructions to the point of its second rise.

2. Remove an avocado-size portion of dough.

3. Dust a work surface with the dark cocoa powder. Stretch the small portion of dough over the cocoa powder and work the cocoa into the dough until it is completely incorporated and the dough has changed color.

4. Let both doughs proof, covered, as directed.

Vegetable Preparation

1. Prepare two pieces of parchment about the size of your intended focaccia and lay them on two 18 x 13-inch (46 x 33 cm) baking sheets. Coat the parchment on one of the sheets with 1 tablespoon of the oil.

2. To make the chicks, cut a long slice that is ¾ inch (2 cm) thick from the yellow squash and lay it flat on a cutting board, peel side up. Cut 3 circles using the circle cookie cutter. Cut a small triangular notch from each circle from one side into the center to make space for the beak.

3. Cut ¼-inch-thick (6 mm) rounds from the orange carrot, then cut out three ½-inch-long (1 cm) narrow triangles for the beaks to fit in the notches of the yellow-squash chicks.

4. Press 2 black peppercorns into the top half of each of the chicks for eyes and a carrot beak in the notch. Set aside.

5. Prep the peppers and red onion for cutting out shapes (see Making the Cut on pages 23 and 24). Use the oval cookie cutter to cut out 6 eggs in different colors from the peppers and 2 purple eggs from the red onion. Also cut out 2 eggs from the green part of the leek.

6. Slice the carrot into ¼-inch-thick (6 mm) rounds and prep the potato for cutting out shapes (see Making the Cut on page 24). Use the flower cookie cutter to cut out shapes from them and the remaining parts of the peppers and red onion.

7. Cut six 2-inch-long (5 cm) stems that are ¼ inch wide (6 mm) from the green part of the leek. Lay the greenest part of the leek lengthwise on a cutting board, then cut out four 3-inch-long (7.5 cm) leaf shapes with a paring knife.

8. Make a bow from the white part of the leek by cutting three thick strips and one circle. Trim the edges of the strips to resemble a ribbon.

9. To make 2 calla lilies, follow the directions for making a calla lily from a leek layer (see Making the Cut on page 23). Cut 2 narrow slices of orange pepper, about 2 inches (5 cm) long, and fray them along the sides. Place these in the notches of the calla lilies.

10. Use the remaining pieces of the colored vegetables to make about thirty-two ½-inch (5 cm) diamond shapes.

11. Move all the vegetables to the unoiled baking sheet, keeping things separate and organized by color and sizes for ease of use during the decorating process.

Oven Preparation

Thirty minutes prior to baking, move the oven rack to the middle and preheat the oven to 450°F (230°C; gas mark 8), allowing time for the oven to come to full temperature.

Shaping and Decorating

1. Shape the dough while dimpling it (page 17) into an egg shape, about 15 inches (38 cm) long and 9 inches (23 cm) wide, leaving some space on the sides of the baking sheet. If the dough is springing back, allow it to rest for 5 to 8 minutes. The dough will be supple and ready for shaping again.

2. Coat the dough with the remaining 2 tablespoons oil.

3. Begin with the lattice and braid trim. Using a rolling pin, roll out the smaller, dark piece of dough on a lightly floured surface to an 8 x 4-inch (20 x 10 cm) rectangle. Using a ruler and a pizza cutter or paring knife, cut six ¼-inch-wide (6 mm) strips lengthwise for the braiding. Set aside. If you do not have a lattice cutter, then continue to cut long strips, also ¼ inch (6 mm) wide. (Follow the directions on page 26 for latticework.) Lay the lattice on the dough along the wider base of the egg shape.

4. Follow the directions on page 27 for making 2 simple three-strand braids. Trim the top edge of the lattice basket with braided dough. Add more braided dough from the center of the basket trim up to the top of the egg-shaped dough for a handle. Tuck any loose strands under the focaccia dough.

5. Begin placing decorations on the dough. Start with the leek stems and leaves. As you place each stem, "lock" it in place by pushing it down into the dough with a chopstick. To set them in place, use the back end of the chopstick to push the stems down into the dough deeply, at the top and bottom and a few spots in between.

6. Place the 3 chicks on the top half of the dough.

7. Fill in the rest of the space with the egg and flower cutouts.

8. Place the 2 calla lilies near the left center of the basket standing tall.

9. Fill most of the diamond-shaped holes in the latticework with the diamond vegetable cutouts.

10. Lastly, place the ribbon made from leeks on the basket handle in the center.

11. Once you have finished decorating, survey the surface and deflate any large air bubbles with a toothpick or skewer, leaving smaller ones intact (docking). Using piano-style finger motions, gently dimple the dough again. Ultimately, you want to see an uneven bubbly texture, about 1½ to 2 inches (4 to 5 cm) thick in various spots. If the focaccia is flat, allow it to rest for 8 to 10 minutes in a warm, draft-free place.

Baking

1. Just before placing your focaccia in the oven, check the decorations to be sure they are all snug. Secure any that look to be popping off, using a chopstick, skewer, or your fingers.

2. Add finishing salt (if using) and place the focaccia on the middle rack of the oven.

3. Bake for 8 minutes at 450°F (230°C; gas mark 8). Reduce the heat to 375°F (190°C; gas mark 5) and check the decorations again. If any are popping off, coerce them back into the dough by gently and carefully poking down. You don't want to burn yourself. Bake for 10 to 16 more minutes, until the focaccia is golden brown and crisp on the edges.

4. Remove from the oven and let cool for at least 5 to 10 minutes before cutting.

Thanksgiving Cornucopia

This attractive focaccia filled with colorful vegetables and flowers will complement any fall feast.

YIELD: 1 FOCACCIA

1 recipe for Basic White Focaccia (page 30) or Basic Whole Wheat Focaccia (page 34)

3 tablespoons extra-virgin olive or neutral oil, divided

1 teaspoon lemon juice

Bowl of ice water

4 leaves sage

6 leaves basil

4 sprigs parsley

1 red mini sweet pepper

2 yellow mini sweet peppers

2 orange mini sweet peppers

1 small red onion

4 grape tomatoes

1 pitted black olive

2 baby corns

1 mini purple potato

1 small leek

1 scallion (about 7 inches, or 18 cm, long)

Flour, for dusting

Finishing salt, to taste (optional)

Special Tools

Small flower-shaped cookie cutter

Dough Preparation

Prepare the dough according to the recipe instructions to the point of its second rise.

Vegetable Preparation

1. Prepare two pieces of parchment about the size of your intended focaccia and lay them on two 18 x 13-inch (46 x 33 cm) baking sheets. Coat the parchment on one of the sheets with 1 tablespoon of the oil.

2. Add the lemon juice to the bowl of ice water to keep the greens bright. Place the sage, basil, and parsley in the ice water.

3. Cut out flower petals from one each of the yellow and orange mini peppers and from the red onion (see Making the Cut on pages 23 and 24). Create a splayed flower from the red mini pepper (see Making the Cut on page 23), then place in the ice water to help it open up more.

4. Slice the grape tomatoes in half and place, seed sides down, on a paper towel to drain any excess liquid. Pat the olive dry. Cut the olive and the baby corn in half lengthwise.

5. Cut out 4 or 5 flowers with the cookie cutter from the purple potato.

6. Make a shallow, lengthwise slit down one side of the leek, then peel off and discard the outer layer. Carefully separate out 3 or 4 layers and wash under cold running water to remove dirt and sand. Make a feather shape about 4 inches (10 cm) long and make slits on each side of each layer for fringed edges.

7. Slice the scallion lengthwise into a few layers, leaving the bottom intact.

8. Move all the vegetables to the unoiled baking sheet, keeping things separate and organized by color and sizes for ease of use during the decorating process. Remove the greens from the ice water and dry them well before placing on the baking sheet.

Oven Preparation

Thirty minutes prior to baking, move the oven rack to the middle and preheat the oven to 450°F (230°C; gas mark 8), allowing time for the oven to come to full temperature.

Shaping

1. Cut off a golf ball–size piece of dough and set aside. Shape the larger piece of dough while dimpling it (page 17) into a cornucopia shape. It's easiest to make this shape by placing the parchment with the dough directly on the work surface. Start by shaping it into a 12 x 8-inch (30 x 20 cm) rectangle. Take the top-left corner of the dough and begin to twist, pulling outward at the same time. Squeeze toward the center with both hands, narrowing the shape a bit to look like a horn. Twist up the tail piece into a curl at the narrow end. This will give the effect of a twisted-horn cornucopia, leaving an oval about 10 inches (25 cm) in size to place the decorations on. If the dough is springing back, allow it to rest for 5 to 8 minutes. The dough will be supple and ready for shaping again.

2. Using your hands, roll the smaller piece of reserved dough into a 24-inch-long (61 cm) rope, or until the strand is about ¼ inch (6 mm) thick. Cut off two 4-inch (10 cm) pieces from the rope and set aside. With the remaining piece, fold it in half and twist it about 8 times to give it a braid-like look. Spritz with water and place along the top of the oval. Pinch in the ends under the flattened cornucopia dough to give definition to the opening of the cornucopia.

3. With the two 4-inch (10 cm) pieces, create wheat stalks. Roll them slightly to taper each end, then using kitchen scissors, snip little notches at the tops and along both sides, about 1 inch (2.5 cm) down the stem. Spritz the dough stalks with water, then lay them on the cornucopia.

4. Coat the dough with the remaining 2 tablespoons oil.

Decorating

1. Place the parchment and shaped dough back on the baking sheet. Turn the baking sheet so that the oval is closest to you. The decorations will be tightly placed and slightly overlapping.

2. Place an olive half on the right side of the oval and surround it with yellow pepper petals to make a flower.

3. On the bottom-left side, create a flower with a tomato center surrounded by red onion petals.

4. Make a partial or whole flower with the orange pepper petals on the bottom center, depending on the space. Use an olive half for the center of a whole flower.

5. Place the parsley and basil all over the oval.

6. Place the feathered leek along the top right of the oval and add the baby corn halves.

7. Lay the scallion above the braid with its stem going down into the cornucopia opening. Spread the layers out across the horn, then place the sage leaves along one of the scallion layers.

8. Fill the remaining space with potato flowers and tomato halves.

9. Allow the focaccia to rest for 10 to 15 minutes in a warm, draft-free place after decorating. The shape should puff up nicely. Survey the surface and deflate any large air bubbles with a toothpick or skewer, leaving smaller ones intact (docking). Using piano-style finger motions, gently dimple the dough again. Ultimately, you want to see an uneven bubbly texture, about 1½ to 2 inches (4 to 5 cm) thick in various spots. If the focaccia is flat, allow it to rest for 8 to 10 minutes in a warm, draft-free place.

Baking

1. Just before placing your focaccia in the oven, check the decorations to be sure they are all snug. Secure any that look to be popping off, using a chopstick, skewer, or your fingers.

2. Add finishing salt (if using) and place the focaccia on the middle rack of the oven.

3. Bake for 8 minutes at 450°F (230°C; gas mark 8). Reduce the heat to 375°F (190°C; gas mark 5) and check the decorations again. If any are popping off, coerce them back into the dough by gently and carefully poking down. You don't want to burn yourself. Bake for 10 to 16 more minutes, until the focaccia is golden brown and crisp on the edges.

4. Remove from the oven and let cool for at least 5 to 10 minutes before cutting.

Christmas Tree

Decorating a focaccia tree is very much like decorating the real thing, so make this pull-apart bread for a tree decorating party.

YIELD: 1 FOCACCIA

1 recipe for Basic White Focaccia (page 30) or Basic Whole Wheat Focaccia (page 34)

2 tablespoons extra-virgin olive or neutral oil, divided

2 red mini sweet peppers

2 yellow mini sweet peppers

2 orange mini sweet peppers

1 medium red onion

1 mini purple potato

2 teaspoons flaxseeds or white sesame seeds

¾ to 1 cup (150 to 200 g) Basil Pesto (page 169)

Finishing salt, to taste (optional)

Special Tools

Mini circle cookie cutter

Medium star-shaped cookie cutter

Dough Preparation

Prepare the dough according to the recipe instructions to the point of its second rise.

Vegetable Preparation

1. Prepare two pieces of parchment about the size of your intended focaccia and lay them on two 18 x 13-inch (46 x 33 cm) baking sheets. Coat the parchment on one of the sheets with 1 tablespoon of the oil.

2. Prep the peppers, onion, and potato for cutting out shapes (see Making the Cut on pages 23 and 24).

3. Use the circle cookie cutter to cut out circles from these veggies. You will need about 6 circles of each color. Cut out the star to top the tree with the star cookie cutter from one-half of a yellow pepper.

4. Move all the vegetables to the unoiled baking sheet, keeping things separate and organized by color and sizes for ease of use during the decorating process. Place the seeds on the baking sheet too.

Oven Preparation

Thirty minutes prior to baking, move the oven rack to the middle and preheat the oven to 450°F (230°C; gas mark 8), allowing time for the oven to come to full temperature.

Shaping

1. Shape the dough while dimpling it (page 17) into a basic Christmas tree shape—a triangle with a rounded top and a trunk at the bottom—by gently pulling and squeezing the dough. If the dough is springing back allow it to rest for 5 to 8 minutes. The dough will be supple and ready for shaping again. The dough will continue to relax as you decorate.

2. Coat the dough with the remaining 1 tablespoon oil, leaving the areas where the Basil Pesto will be spread uncoated.

Decorating

1. Evenly spread the basil pesto over the surface of the dough, just leaving the rounded edge at the top uncovered for the star.

2. Use a paring knife or bench knife to make 1-inch-wide (2.5 cm) horizontal slices up each side of the triangle shape, leaving 1 inch (2.5 cm) of uncut dough running down the center.

3. Starting from the bottom, turn each strip of dough slightly, giving it a twist and overlapping with the next one—these are your "branches."

4. Sprinkle flaxseeds on the trunk area to give the impression of wood.

5. Decorate the tree with the colored circle cutouts, finishing with the yellow star at the top.

6. Let the dough rest, covered, in a warm, draft-free place for 5 or 10 minutes to spring back. No need for re-dimpling at this point; this is a pull-apart focaccia.

Baking

1. Just before placing your focaccia in the oven, check the decorations to be sure they are all snug. Secure any that look to be popping off, using a chopstick, skewer, or your fingers.

2. Add finishing salt (if using) and place the focaccia on the middle rack of the oven.

3. Bake for 8 minutes at 450°F (230°C; gas mark 8). Reduce the heat to 375°F (190°C; gas mark 5) and check the decorations again. If any are popping off, coerce them back into the dough by gently and carefully poking down. You don't want to burn yourself. Bake for 10 to 16 more minutes, until the focaccia is golden brown and crisp on the edges.

4. Remove from the oven and let cool for at least 5 to 10 minutes before pulling apart.

Cinnamon Star

Bursting onto the scene for a holiday breakfast is this star that pulls apart into cinnamon buns. It is layered with cinnamon and has a center overflowing with sweet cream cheese for dipping.

YIELD: 1 FOCACCIA

1 recipe for Sweet Focaccia (page 41)

Flour, for dusting

1 tablespoon plus 1 teaspoon neutral oil

1 cup (208 g) Cinnamon Filling (page 167)

Egg wash (1 egg mixed with ¼ cup, or 60 ml, water) or whole milk, for brushing (optional)

1 tablespoon sparkling sugar (optional)

1 cup (230 g) Sweet Lemon Cream Dip (see Variation on page 167)

1¼ cups (120 g) toasted chopped walnuts (optional)

Special Tools

1 (4-ounce, or 120-ml) ramekin (3 inches, or 6 cm, in size)

Dough Preparation

1. Prepare the sweet dough according to the recipe directions. After a full second rise, turn the dough out onto a lightly floured work surface. Pat the dough into a disc, then use a bowl scraper or bench knife to cut the disc in half. Cut each half in half again so that you have 4 equal-size pieces.

2. Roll each piece into a ball and allow to rest, covered with a tea towel, on the floured surface for 10 minutes.

Oven Preparation

Thirty minutes prior to baking, move the oven rack to the middle and preheat the oven to 350°F (180°C; gas mark 4), allowing time for the oven to come to full temperature.

Shaping

1. Line an 18 x 13-inch (46 x 33 cm) baking sheet with parchment. Coat the parchment with 1 tablespoon of the oil.

2. Using a rolling pin, roll out the first dough ball to an 8-inch (20 cm) disc on a lightly floured surface. Place the disc on the prepared baking sheet and coat it with some of the cinnamon filling, leaving a ½-inch (1 cm) gap around the edge uncoated.

3. Roll out the next ball of dough to the same size. Place this over the cinnamon-covered disc on the baking sheet. Coat with cinnamon filling, leaving a ½-inch (1 cm) gap around the edge uncoated again. Repeat with the third ball of dough.

Roll out the fourth and final dough ball to an 8-inch (20 cm) disc and place it on top of the layered dough circles, but do not coat this layer with cinnamon filling.

4. Prepare the ramekin by cutting a small piece of parchment slightly larger than the base of the ramekin. Lightly oil both sides of the parchment paper with the remaining 1 teaspoon oil and lay it in the center of the layered dough circles. Use a ruler for accuracy. Press the ramekin into the dough on top of the parchment paper to create a slight divot, ¾ to 1 inch (2 to 2.5 cm) deep.

5. With the ramekin placed in the center of the dough, using a paring or bench knife, begin by making 4 equal-size cuts, slicing from the ramekin to the edge of the dough. Slice each quarter in half lengthwise, and then slice each in half lengthwise again so that you have 16 slices total.

6. Use both hands to pick up the first 2 strips of dough from the end and pinch slightly to seal the ends. Twist each piece 3 times outward in the opposite direction of each other, then bring the ends together. Pinch to seal the strips together and tuck loose ends slightly under if necessary. Repeat this process with the rest of the layered strips until you have an eight-point star.

7. Gently press the ramekin down one last time, cover the star, and let rest in a warm, draft-free place for 20 minutes.

Baking

1. If you like to add a little twinkle to your star, gently brush the dough with egg wash and sprinkle with the sparkling sugar.

2. Place the focaccia on the middle rack of the preheated oven, leaving the oven-safe ramekin in the middle. This will help create a well for the sweet lemon cream.

3. Bake for 28 to 34 minutes, until golden.

4. After removing from the oven, carefully remove the ramekin and piece of parchment and allow to cool slightly before placing the sweet lemon cream in the middle for dipping (see Note). The walnuts (if using) can be served on the side in a small ramekin or sprinkled over the sweet lemon cream. Serve immediately on a beautiful platter.

NOTE

To make a day in advance, fully bake the cinnamon star, then, after it has cooled completely, wrap the whole baking sheet with plastic wrap. Keep the lemon sweet cream separate in the refrigerator. The next day, preheat the oven to 350°F (180°C; gas mark 4), unwrap the star, and bake for 5 minutes. Remove and follow the directions above for serving.

Game Day

This focaccia is not only great for serving at a party for the Big Game, but it can be altered to fit a number of sporting events. Change up the ball (see Variation on page 161) for a wonderful sport-themed birthday bread.

YIELD: 1 FOCACCIA

1 recipe for Basic White Focaccia (page 30) or Basic Whole Wheat Focaccia (page 34)

1 tablespoon dark cocoa powder

2 tablespoons extra-virgin olive or neutral oil, divided

1 small green bell pepper

1 small red bell pepper

1 small yellow bell pepper

1 small orange bell pepper

1 medium red onion

1 large leek (10 to 11 inches, or 25 to 28 cm, long)

1 large white carrot, peeled

1 large purple carrot, peeled

1 whole medium roasted red bell pepper (see page 25 for how to roast your own)

2 pimiento-stuffed green olives

2 pitted black olives

1 tablespoon black sesame or poppy seeds

½ cup (100 g) Basil Pesto (page 169)

Finishing salt, to taste (optional)

Special Tools

Mini circle cookie cutter

Dough Preparation

1. Prepare the dough according to the recipe instructions to the point of its second rise.

2. Cut off a golf ball–size piece of dough. Dust a work surface with the dark cocoa powder. Roll and knead the small portion of dough in the cocoa powder until the dough is dark brown and the cocoa powder is incorporated.

3. Let both doughs proof, covered, as directed.

Vegetable Preparation

1. Prepare two pieces of parchment about the size of your intended focaccia and lay them on two 18 x 13-inch (46 x 33 cm) baking sheets. Coat the parchment on one of the sheets with 1 tablespoon of the oil.

2. Prep the peppers and red onion for cutting out shapes (see Making the Cut on pages 23 and 24).

3. Make a shallow, lengthwise slit down one side of the leek, then peel off and discard the outer layer. Carefully separate out a few layers and wash under cold running water to remove dirt and sand.

4. Use the circle cookie cutter to make about 50 circles from the peppers, onion, and green part of the leek for the spectators.

5. Separate out some white layers from the leek and cut them into 3 strips that are 10 inches (25 cm) long and ¼ inch (6 mm) wide for the lines on the football field.

6. Cut number shapes from the white carrot to indicate yard lines. Also cut small thin strips from the carrot for laces for the football. Use a julienne peeler to cut the purple carrot into thin strips for bleacher dividers.

7. Cut the roasted red pepper into two 4-inch-long (10 cm) and two 3-inch-long (7.5 cm) strips, all ½ inch (1 cm) wide, for the goal post.

8. Pat the green and black olives dry. Slice the olives into about 10 thin rounds crosswise.

9. Move all the vegetables to the unoiled baking sheet, keeping things separate and organized by color and sizes for ease of use during the decorating process. Place the seeds on the baking sheet too.

Oven Preparation

Thirty minutes prior to baking, move the oven rack to the middle and preheat the oven to 450°F (230°C; gas mark 8), allowing time for the oven to come to full temperature.

Shaping and Decorating

1. On the oiled baking sheet, shape your uncolored dough while dimpling it (page 17) into a rectangular dough "canvas," about 16 x 11 inches (41 x 28 cm). Shape the smaller, dark piece of dough into a football shape. Coat both doughs with the remaining 1 tablespoon oil, leaving the area where the Basil Pesto will be spread uncoated.

2. Spread the basil pesto over the bottom half of the dough. Sprinkle a 2-inch-wide (5 cm) line of black sesame seeds just above the pesto.

3. Create a stadium background on the top half of the dough by placing the purple carrot strips as bleacher dividers. Lay them 1 inch (2.5 cm) apart horizontally. As you place each strip, "lock" it in place by pushing it down into the dough with a chopstick. To set the strip in place, use the back end of the chopstick to push it down into the dough deeply, at the top and bottom and a few spots in between.

4. Place a variety of colored circles among the bleacher dividers to represent the fans.

5. Lay the white strips of leek horizontally across the pesto for the lines on the football field, 1½ to 2 inches (4 to 5 cm) apart. Place the carrot numbers along the left side of the football field.

6. Pat the roasted red pepper strips dry, then form them into a goal post in the middle of the dough.

7. Place the dough football on the goal post and lay the white carrot strips on top of the football for the laces.

8. Once you have finished decorating, survey the surface and deflate any large air bubbles with a toothpick or skewer, leaving smaller ones intact (docking). Using piano-style finger motions, gently dimple the dough again. Ultimately, you want to see an uneven bubbly texture, about 1½ to 2 inches (4 to 5 cm) thick in various spots. If the focaccia is flat, allow it to rest for 8 to 10 minutes in a warm, draft-free place.

Baking

1. Just before placing your focaccia in the oven, check the decorations to be sure they are all snug. Secure any that look to be popping off, using the chopstick, a skewer, or your fingers.

2. Add finishing salt (if using) and place the focaccia on the middle rack of the oven.

3. Bake for 8 minutes at 450°F (230°C; gas mark 8). Reduce the heat to 375°F (190°C; gas mark 5) and check the decorations again. If any are popping off, coerce them back into the dough by gently and carefully poking down. You don't want to burn yourself. Bake for 10 to 16 more minutes, until the focaccia is golden brown and crisp on the edges.

4. Remove from the oven and let cool for at least 5 to 10 minutes before cutting.

VARIATION: OTHER SPORTS

Soccer: To create a soccer ball, slice a 3-inch (7.5 cm) ring from the center of a red onion, removing the interior portion of the ring. Lay the ring on the dough and sprinkle the interior lightly with 1 teaspoon of poppy or black sesame seeds. Cut hexagon shapes from the flesh of a zucchini or white carrot and place them in the onion on top of the seeds to fill in the ball. Use a julienne cutter to cut carrot strips to create a lattice for the goal netting.

Baseball: Make a baseball bat from a yellow squash and a baseball from a roasted red pepper that has been frayed on either side. Place the baseball in a ¼-inch-thick (6 mm) onion ring. Place the home plate at the bottom of the focaccia made from the white part of a leek or a zucchini cut into ½-inch-thick (1 cm) slices.

Hockey: Make a hockey stick out of zucchini and a puck from a black olive. Use a julienne cutter to cut carrot strips to create a lattice for the goal netting.

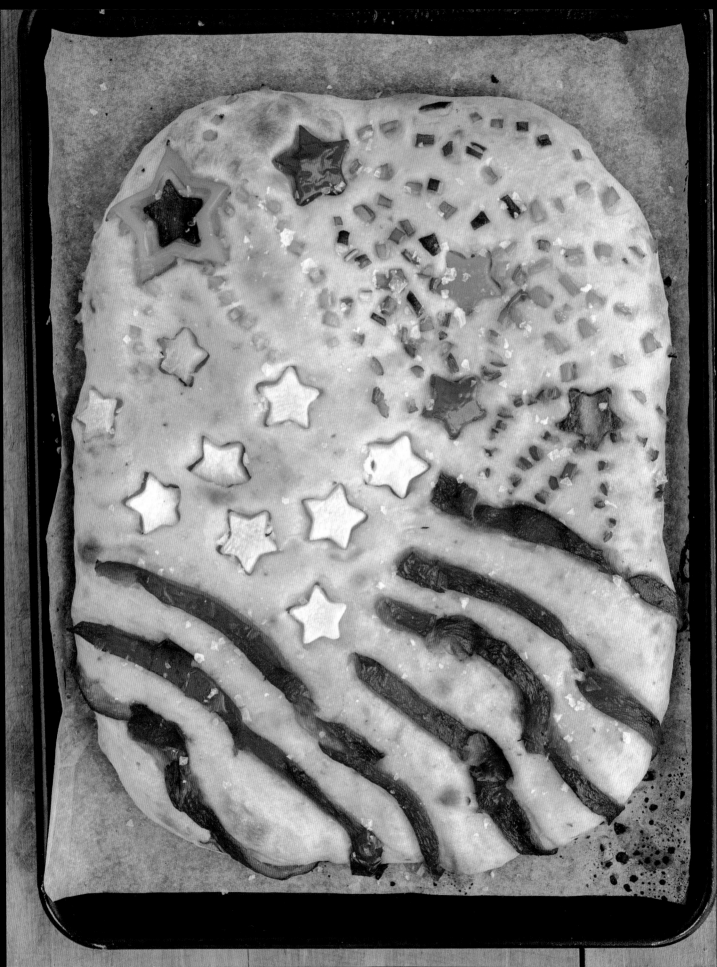

Celebration Fireworks

Whether it is a celebration of New Year's Eve, Fourth of July, Diwali, or Bastille Day, there is nothing that excites more brightly than fireworks. Your guests will delight in this festive, colorful focaccia.

YIELD: 1 FOCACCIA

1 recipe for Basic White Focaccia (page 30) or Basic Whole Wheat Focaccia (page 34)

3 tablespoons extra-virgin olive or neutral oil, divided

1 small green bell pepper

2 red mini sweet peppers

2 yellow mini sweet peppers

2 orange mini sweet peppers

2 small, firm white potatoes or white turnips, peeled

1 mini purple potato

1 large whole roasted red pepper (see page 25 for how to roast your own)

1 small red onion

Finishing salt, to taste (optional)

Special Tools

Small and medium star-shaped cookie cutters

Dough Preparation

Prepare the dough according to the recipe instructions to its second rise.

Vegetable Preparation

1. Prepare two pieces of parchment about the size of your intended focaccia and lay them on two 18 x 13-inch (46 x 33 cm) baking sheets. Coat the parchment on one of the sheets with 1 tablespoon of the oil.

2. Prep the green bell pepper and half of the mini peppers for cutting out shapes (see Making the Cut on page 23). Use the cookie cutters to cut out 4 small and medium star shapes from the peppers in various colors.

3. Prep the white and purple potatoes for cutting out shapes (see Making the Cut on page 24), then cut out 2 or 3 small stars from the purple potato and 9 or 10 small stars from the white potatoes.

4. Cut the roasted red pepper lengthwise into fourteen ¼-inch-wide (6 mm) strips.

5. Cut the remaining pepper pieces and red onion into ¼-inch (6 mm) rectangles so that you have a bunch of them in all colors.

6. Move all the vegetables to the unoiled baking sheet, keeping things separate and organized by color and sizes for ease of use during the decorating process.

Oven Preparation

Thirty minutes prior to baking, move the oven rack to the middle and preheat the oven to 450°F (230°C; gas mark 8), allowing time for the oven to come to full temperature.

Shaping and Decorating

1. On the oiled baking sheet, shape your dough while dimpling it (page 17) into a rectangular dough "canvas," about 16 x 11 inches (41 x 28 cm), then coat it with the remaining 2 tablespoons oil.

2. Begin by laying down the red pepper strips. Place the first strip at an angle on the bottom-left corner of the dough, shaped into a flowing line. Lay down 2 more wavy lines across the bottom, above the first one, then lay the remaining 4 strips at an angle just halfway up the dough on the right side, leaving the space on the left open for the small white stars.

3. Place the white stars in random spots on the left next to and above the pepper strips.

4. Place the colorful pepper and potato stars over the rest of the dough.

5. Give these stars sparkly tails with the tiny rectangles of colored vegetables spraying out from the stars, crowding the top of the dough with lots of color.

6. Once you have finished decorating, survey the surface and deflate any large air bubbles with a toothpick or skewer, leaving smaller ones intact (docking). Using piano-style finger motions, gently dimple the dough again. Ultimately, you want to see an uneven bubbly texture, about 1½ to 2 inches (4 to 5 cm) thick in various spots. If the focaccia is flat, allow it to rest for 8 to 10 minutes in a warm, draft-free place.

Baking

1. Just before placing your focaccia in the oven, check the decorations to be sure they are all snug. Secure any that look to be popping off, using a chopstick, skewer, or your fingers.

2. Add finishing salt (if using) and place the focaccia on the middle rack of the oven.

3. Bake for 8 minutes at 450°F (230°C; gas mark 8). Reduce the heat to 375°F (190°C; gas mark 5) and check the decorations again. If any are popping off, coerce them back into the dough by gently and carefully poking down. You don't want to burn yourself. Bake for 10 to 16 more minutes, until the focaccia is golden brown and crisp on the edges.

4. Remove from the oven and let cool for at least 5 to 10 minutes before cutting.

Additional Recipes

Chocolate Hazelnut Filling

YIELD: 16 OUNCES (454 G)

¾ cup (100 g) unsalted hazelnuts, roasted (see below for roasting directions)

1 cup (160 g) semisweet chocolate chips

3 tablespoons brown sugar

1 tablespoon cocoa powder

½ teaspoon kosher salt

3 tablespoons butter, softened

1 tablespoon hazelnut liqueur or 2 teaspoons vanilla extract

Directions

1. Place all the ingredients in a food processor or blender and pulse until fine.

2. Use a spatula to transfer the mixture to an airtight container with a lid. Refrigerate until ready to use.

3. The filling can be refrigerated for 2 weeks.

HOW TO ROAST HAZELNUTS

Preheat the oven to 350°F (180°C; gas mark 4). Spread out the hazelnuts on a parchment-lined baking sheet. Bake, on the middle rack, for 10 to 15 minutes, shaking the pan every 5 minutes for even roasting. Toast until golden brown and you can smell the fragrant warm smell. Remove from the oven right away and wrap the nuts in a clean dish towel. Let cool slightly for 3 minutes wrapped in the towel. Rub the towel around on a hard surface, rolling back and forth to remove some of the hazelnut skin. You won't get all the skin off, but this stage is still worth doing.

Cinnamon Filling

YIELD: 16 OUNCES (454 G)

5 tablespoons unsalted butter, softened

2 tablespoons ground cinnamon (use Ceylon cinnamon for best results)

⅓ cup (65 g) sugar

2 tablespoons packed light brown sugar

2 teaspoons all-purpose flour

1 teaspoon ground cardamom (optional)

Pinch of salt

Directions

1. In a medium bowl, whisk together all the ingredients until well blended. Use a spatula to transfer the mixture to an airtight container with a lid.

2. The filling can be refrigerated for 2 weeks or frozen for 2 months. Let it come to room temperature for easy spreading.

Sweet Lemon Cream

YIELD: 11 OUNCES (310 G)

4 ounces (113 g) good-quality cream cheese, at room temperature

1 egg

½ cup (100 g) sugar

1 tablespoon all-purpose flour

Zest of 1 lemon

½ teaspoon vanilla extract

Pinch salt

Directions

1. In a medium bowl or mixer bowl, combine all the ingredients and mix on medium speed with an electric mixer until smooth and creamy, scraping down the sides periodically with a spatula so that it is well blended. The cream will have a thick pudding consistency.

2. Use a spatula to transfer the mixture to an airtight container with a lid. Refrigerate until ready to use.

3. Freeze leftovers or bake in pie pan at 350°F (180°C; gas mark 4) for 20 minutes for a creamy treat.

VARIATION: SWEET LEMON CREAM DIP

To make a dip, eliminate the egg and flour when blending all the ingredients, then refrigerate until ready to use.

Evergreen Sauce

YIELD: ABOUT 1 QUART (1 L)

7 ounces (198 g) curly kale (8 to 10 leaves)

8 ounces (227 g) baby spinach

1 cup (70 g) lightly packed leaves fresh basil

Zest of 1 small lemon

1 tablespoon freshly squeezed lemon juice

3 tablespoons (45 ml) extra-virgin olive oil

4 or 5 cloves garlic

2 ounces (60 g) cream cheese

1 ounce (30 g) feta or other strong hard cheese (see Note)

½ teaspoon kosher salt

½ cup (120 ml) hot water

Directions

1. Place the kale, spinach, and basil in a food processor or blender, with the kale at the bottom, the basil at the top, and the spinach in between. (If you need room to fit them all, run the processor for a few seconds, then add the remaining greens.) Pulse 8 to 10 times to a pulpy consistency.

2. Add the lemon zest and lemon juice and pulse to blend. Leave the food processor blender as is.

3. In a small skillet, heat the olive oil until hot. Turn off the heat and add the garlic cloves. The garlic will get slightly tender as the oil cools and add some sweetness.

4. Pour the oil and garlic into the food processor or blender and add the cheeses and salt. Pulse a couple of times with the lid on.

5. Slowly add the hot water. Depending on how much moisture is in the greens and cheese, you may not need to use the whole amount, or you may need a little more. Ideally you want a thick green sauce that is spreadable and stays on a spoon when held upside down.

6. Spoon the sauce into an airtight container with a lid. Refrigerate until ready to use.

7. The sauce can be refrigerated for 3 days or frozen for 1 month.

NOTE

If you are using feta in brine, be sure to rinse it and pat dry.

Basil Pesto

YIELD: 10 OUNCES (283 G)

2 or 3 cloves garlic

1¼ cups (70 g) leaves fresh basil

½ cup (120 ml) extra-virgin olive oil

½ cup (50 g) grated Parmesan

½ teaspoon kosher salt (or to taste, depending on the quality of the Parmesan)

¼ cup (35 g) pine nuts (or walnuts or butternuts) (optional)

Directions

1. Place the garlic in a food processor or blender fitted with the blade attachment. Add the basil leaves, then pour in the olive oil, evenly distributing it. Pulse 8 to 12 times, scraping down the sides periodically with a spatula, until well blended. Add the Parmesan and salt. Pulse again, 6 to 8 times, scraping down the sides periodically with a spatula, until well blended. Add the pine nuts (if using) and pulse 5 or 6 more times, leaving some pine nuts whole and some chopped.

2. Spoon the pesto into an airtight container with a lid. It can be frozen for 2 months.

Sun-Dried Tomato Pesto

YIELD: 8 OUNCES (227 G)

3 or 4 cloves garlic

1 cup (80 g) sun-dried tomatoes (halves work best)

3 tablespoons extra-virgin olive oil

2 tablespoons water

½ cup (50 g) grated Parmesan

¼ cup (35 g) mild nuts (such as pine, walnut, or hazelnut) (optional)

Ground black pepper, to taste

½ teaspoon kosher salt (or to taste, depending on the quality of the Parmesan)

Directions

1. Place the garlic, sun-dried tomatoes, olive oil, and water in a food processor or blender fitted with the blade attachment. Pulse 6 to 8 times to a pulpy consistency, scraping down the sides periodically with a spatula. Add the Parmesan and nuts and pulse 4 or 5 times to blend, leaving small pieces of sun-dried tomato. Season with the black pepper and salt.

2. Spoon the pesto into an airtight container with a lid. It can be frozen for 2 months.

Quick-Pickled Vegetables

YIELD: 1 (1-QUART, OR 946-ML) WIDE-MOUTH CANNING JAR

VEGETABLES

2 cups (350 g) fresh vegetables (such as cabbage, carrots, beans, asparagus, onions, beets, etc.)

Your favorite fresh herbs (such as rosemary, thyme, garlic, etc.)

BRINE

1¼ cups (300 ml) water

¾ cup (180 ml) vinegar (use apple cider, rice, wine, or white; do not use balsamic)

1½ tablespoons kosher salt

1 to 2 tablespoons granulated sugar (depending on how sweet you like it)

1 tablespoon pickling spice (or make your own combination)

3 fresh bay leaves

Directions

1. Clean the jar, lid, and a funnel and lay out on a kitchen towel. This will be your work surface as well. If you don't have a canning funnel, no worries; just place the jars in your sink and fill the jars there to avoid too much mess.

2. To prep the vegetables: Peel, cut, and blanch the vegetables. For firm vegetables, such as carrots, beets, and celery, blanch them in a pot of boiling water for 8 minutes. For onions and cabbage, blanch for 3 minutes. Drain the produce and pack tightly into the jar, leaving a ½-inch (1 cm) gap at the top of the jar.

3. To make the brine: Place all the brine ingredients in a 2-quart (2 L) pot, bring to a boil, and boil for about 5 minutes, until the salt and sugar have dissolved. Remove from the heat, transfer the bay leaves to the jar with the vegetables, and pour the brine over the vegetables in the jar, leaving a ½-inch (1 cm) gap at the top.

4. Place the lid on the jar and give the jar a tap on the kitchen towel to remove any air bubbles—be careful, as the jar will be hot, so use a towel when handling it. Remove the lid and fill with more brine to cover the vegetables completely.

5. Tightly screw the lid on the jar. Allow the jar to cool for 2 hours at room temperature, then transfer to the refrigerator. The pickled vegetables can be refrigerated for 1 month. (Prolonged refrigeration improves the flavors.)

Index

Acknowledgments

To Jocelyn Filley, who taught me a deep and true appreciation for all the dings, scratches, and faults in a well-used kitchen. They are as unique as the breads coming forth from within. You turned my "whatever, it-is-what-it-is" kitchen into a work of art in photography.

To Erin C. and the team at Quarto, thank you for guiding me through this process and your patience.

To Beth H., Judy W., Diane S., Mary G., and Lisa J., thanks for all your encouragements; lifelong friendships are nourishment to the soul as bread is to the body.

To neighbors Holly and Henry, thanks for taking on the "work" of sampling.

To Thenzel T., Karen H., and Natasha H., who never turn down an opportunity to try bread.

To IGI FARM, thanks for your produce and the opportunity to share.

To the Farm Institute part of the Trustees of Reservations, Lindsey, Lilly and the crew, thank you for the space to teach and the helping hands.

To family, Benjamin and Emily; Camden, Jacob, Gordon, and Sarah; Nick, Annette, Vinnie, Stephanie, and Anthony (FiOH); and Kopac and Culletto families too numerous to list, where the love of family and good bread were tantamount.

To the little ones, Aurora and Ella, I look forward to passing on baking memories with you just as generations before.

About the Author

Theresa (Teri) Culletto, also known as the Vineyard Baker, unknowingly became a baker's apprentice as a child when she spent summers with her grandmother at her home near the Hudson River in New York and would watch her prepare old-world artisan breads. Over the years, Teri took classes through various outlets increasing her knowledge and feeding her interest in bread baking. Later, her passion for bread baking came to be a means for her family. As a single mother of four sons, Ben, Cam, Jake, and Gordon, the family settled on Martha's Vineyard in 1984, where opening a cottage bakery not only fed the boys but supported their home. It was at this time she became known simply as the "Bread Lady" around the island. The boys would help with packaging and selling at the local farmers market, and it became a real family business. It was after the boys grew and moved away that Teri began teaching baking locally and when the focaccia bread art project began. Who knew years later that it would evolve into a food trend on social media, which opened beautiful new "oven doors," as she likes to say. Focaccia bread art was also a great hit with the students who took the bread baking class.

When not baking, Teri likes reading, mostly cookbooks, of course, growing vegetables and flowers, and taking opportunities to volunteer in her community where and whenever she can. She is also a member of the Bread Bakers Guild of America, a wonderful community of both professional and serious home bakers, where she finds inspiration, support, and opportunities to learn new things.

These days, Teri looks forward to baking with her granddaughters, Aurora and Ella, and still teaches classes that are both fun and inspiring. This book is one more wonderful and creative way to indulge in the world of bread baking. She hopes you will be inspired. You can find her on Instagram @vineyardbaker, and she looks forward to seeing your Beautiful Breads.

Happy baking!